PASSION AND PREJUDICE

Nationalist/Unionist Conflict in Ulster in the 1930s and the Origins of the Irish Association

History should not, and indeed cannot, be written without prejudice. A point of view is not only inevitable, but even necessary. Our conception of persons, places or periods is for instance usually coloured by our environment . . . a child now being educated in Cork has a quite different idea of Irish History from one being educated in Belfast.

J J Horgan
in the foreword to
Parnell to Pearse: Some Recollections and Reflections
(Dublin, 1948)

For more than 50 years it [The Irish Association] has provided a forum where Irish people of all shades of opinion can discuss and reflect on our relationships. We are all greatly in the debt of the many dedicated individuals who have worked quietly and without fanfare over the years to foster networks of human contact and dialogue across self-imposed divides.

Dick Spring
from *The Irish Times*, 6 March 1993
at the Mansion House, Dublin

Published 1993
The Institute of Irish Studies
The Queen's University of Belfast,
Belfast

This book has received support from the Cultural Traditions Programme
of the Community Relations Council, which aims to encourage
acceptance and understanding of cultural diversity.

British Library Cataloguing-in-Publication Data. A catalogue record for
this book is available from the British Library.

ISBN 0 85389 477 9

Printed by W & G Baird Ltd., Antrim
Cover designed by Rodney Miller Associates

Passion and Prejudice

**Nationalist/Unionist Conflict in Ulster in the 1930s
and the Origins of the Irish Association**

Paul Bew

Kenneth Darwin

Gordon Gillespie

The Institute of Irish Studies
The Queen's University of Belfast

ACKNOWLEDGEMENTS

We are deeply grateful to Dr Anthony Malcomson and his staff at the Public Record Office of Northern Ireland for their magnificent help with this project. As a result, the scope of the work has been considerably extended. The families of both General Montgomery and Lord Charlemont were enormously helpful, while Rev. Eric Gallagher kindly allowed us to draw on the papers of Mary ('Molly') McNeill which were in his care. We would like to thank Dr Richard Dunphy of Dundee University for permission to quote from his forthcoming book on Fianna Fail in the interwar years which is to be published by Oxford University Press. Thanks are also due to Dr Mary Harris of the University of North London for permission to quote from her Cambridge Ph.D., shortly to be published by Cork University Press. Finally, Dr Brian Walker generously gave much valuable time to the production of the text.

Paul Bew
Kenneth Darwin
Gordon Gillespie

Belfast, March 1993

CONTENTS

INTRODUCTION

Serious Irish Nationalist–Ulster Unionist dialogue in the twen-
tieth century has been a rare occurrence: exchange of abuse
has been rather more commonplace. When John Hume was
preparing the SDLP's presentation for the Brooke/Mayhew
talks of 1991/2, he had, in fact, to go back to a speech given
by Parnell in Belfast in 1891 before he could find a reasonably
conciliatory authoritative Nationalist analysis of the Unionist
position.[1] Of course, in one sense there has been a complete
mutual understanding. As Sir James Craig famously put it: 'In
the South they boasted of a Catholic State . . . All I boast of is
that we are a Protestant Parliament and a Protestant State.'[2]
But this understanding – sublime though it was – was too subversive of the rights of minorities to last. Recognising this, the
Irish Association for cultural, economic and social relations
was founded in 1938 by Major-General Hugh Montgomery
CB, CMG, DL (Blessingbourne, Co Tyrone).

Montgomery founded the association after a long period
of discussion and correspondence with a close friend,
Viscount Charlemont, and that correspondence is the core of
this publication. The Irish Association is a non-party political
and non-sectarian association with the aim 'to make reason
and goodwill take the place of passion and prejudice in Ireland, north and south'. In the half century and more which
has elapsed since its foundation, the Association has consist-
ently provided the broadest platform for the discussion of the
most pressing and difficult issues of Irish life. Except for those
committed to violence, it has been addressed by the entire
spectrum of Irish opinion: the most senior politicians and
clergymen of the two main Irish traditions have frequently
graced the meetings of the Association. The purpose has been
to keep the channels of communication open even when

mutual distrust – and even dislike – was at its highest. 'The word politics did not occur in the title of the Association but politics are often discussed at our meetings. Our strength consists in being prepared to give every view an airing while scrupulously avoiding actual political involvement.'[3]

What type of men were Montgomery and Charlemont and what motivated them to set up the Irish Association? Montgomery (1871–1954) was educated at Eton and the Royal Military Academy, Sandhurst. He served with the Royal Artillery in the Boer War – alongside James Craig, later to become Prime Minister of Northern Ireland – and in World War I. In both campaigns he was mentioned in dispatches. Among the decorations he held were the Order of St Anne (Third Class), conferred by the Czar of Russia, the Legion of Honour and the Croix de Guerre. After retiring from the army in 1925 he was for many years a member of Tyrone County Council and played a prominent part in the public life of the county. In these respects, Montgomery was not so very different from a number of other Northern Irish country gentlemen with good military records. But in one respect he was very different: he had an acute sense of a complex heritage. Montgomery was the eldest son of Hugh de Fellenburg Montgomery, a senior Liberal Unionist who had founded a non-sectarian school at Fivemiletown. His mother was the eldest daughter of the Rev. John Charles Maude, rector of Enniskillen. He was also a collateral descendant of the Rev. George Montgomery, a brother of that Hugh Montgomery who with James Hamilton had been responsible at the close of the sixteenth century for the planting of Co Down. As a Unionist member of his local council Montgomery pursued whatever measures he could to promote better relations between the two religious communities, even if this led to disputes with erstwhile political colleagues. On 7 June 1930 Montgomery unsuccessfully tried to get Unionist members of Clogher District Council to support the appointment of James Hackett, a Catholic Nationalist, as Deputy Vice-Chairman of the local Board of Guardians.[4] Although Hackett had held the post for the three previous years, Montgomery's proposal that he be reappointed for another term was turned down by the other Unionist members. Montgomery accepted the decision. Despite this, Montgomery received a letter from the solicitor to the South Tyrone Unionist Association three days later which (according to Montgomery) said somewhat breathlessly:

My view is that unless an undertaking is given by you before the appointments on Tuesday that you will well and faithfully carry out your undertaking to vote with the party and further that you will on the making of all appointments to any office vote Unionist and for a Protestant and failing this undertaking by you then that the matter of appointing you to any office be reconsidered.

Montgomery noted that this letter had the authority of neither the President or Secretary of the Association. According to his notes, Montgomery approached the solicitor at the Unionist meeting on 10 June and told him 'that I declined to be either threatened or dictated to by him'. Montgomery also noted that he was subsequently excluded from the membership of the Regional Education Committee of which he had been chairman for five years. He observed that:

The expediency of re-appointing Mr Hackett is of course open to question; but in my opinion his appointment three years ago was justified: on the few occasions on which he has been called upon to take the Chair his conduct has been businesslike and impartial, and the slight concession involved has led to a much more amicable atmosphere in the proceedings of the Board of which Mr Hackett has for many years been a useful member. I submit that I was perfectly within my rights in proposing his re-election. Incidentally I see that a Roman Catholic has been appointed Deputy Vice-Chairman of the neighbouring Union at Lisnaskea.

In her excellent account of the origins of the Irish Association, Mary McNeill writes of its founder:

All his life he carried with him the sense of conflict that the plantation – 'colonisation' in modern parlance – has bequeathed to Ulster, and the knowledge that he and his family were beneficiaries of that conflict. He made no secret of his acceptance of these two inheritances, the one of conflict, the other of position and privilege. It is not too much to say that when he settled at Blessingbourne on his retirement from the army in 1925 his main activities were henceforward directed towards discharging what he felt to be a debt to his dispossessed Catholic countrymen. At the same time there were no less important obligations of position and privilege, of the Anglican tradition in Church and State in which he and his ancestors had been reared, together with the traditions of the British army in which he had served with distinction. He was a staunch and active member of the Church of Ireland and his unrelenting belief in the benefits to Ireland of the British connection led him to join the Unionist party.[5]

This analysis of Montgomery's world view is supported by his grandson, journalist Hugh Massingberd, who wrote:

My earliest memories are of my grandfather's family seat of Blessingbourne in Co Tyrone (a Victorian exercise in the Elizabethan style by F Pepys Cockerell) and its distinctive smell of burning turf, polished wood, damp mackintoshes and homely cooking. I remember Paddy the butler, while serving the potatoes in the dining-room, spotting a pheasant out of the window; he promptly put the dish down and headed purposefully for the terrace. Having bagged the bird, he returned to his duties at table. . . .

My grandfather, Major-General Hugh Montgomery, the visionary founder of the Irish Association for cultural, economic and social relations devoted his life to fighting bigotry. He hailed from the traditional background of the Lowland Scottish planters who colonised Ulster in the early 17th century. But, unlike some of his neighbours, he never lost sight of the true nature of his heritage. 'To my mind before we can tackle the question seriously,' he wrote during the birth pangs of the Irish Association in the 1930s, 'there must be some element of remorse for the sins committed by our forefathers – sins by which many of us are still benefiting – against the ancestors of our Roman Catholic neighbours.'[6]

The letters included in this volume confirm this fundamental truth. It has to be said that Montgomery had a considerably more sensitive, even guilty, conscience than Viscount James Charlemont (1880–1949). Educated at Winchester and commissioned in the Coldstream Guards in 1914, he had previously taken a prominent part in the Ulster Volunteer movement against Home Rule.[7] Charlemont's letters, while full of the spirit of liberalism, are more irreverent than Montgomery's; in particular, they also tend to be more Unionist and less sympathetic to Nationalist grievances. At the time of this correspondence Lord Charlemont was Northern Ire-

land's second Minister of Education (1926–1937). His principles in office were perfectly clear: 'I cannot say how strongly
I object to the idea that a Unionist government is brought in
not only to maintain the Union but also to humour the sectarian prejudices of all Unionists.'[8] He was the one minister
to oppose the gerrymander of Derry in 1936.[9] He was perhaps
a little cynical about the role of Gaelic culture. 'There is no
doubt that the fact that some recognition is given to Irish by
the Ministry has greatly disarmed criticism on the part of
anti-British elements in the population, while the actual
results in spreading a knowledge of the language are
insignificant.'[10] The Nationalist leader Joe Devlin paid a full
public tribute to Charlemont's 'courtesy', 'kindness' and
'good will'.[11] Charlemont's conception of the work of the
Association is clear: 'Its aims were to give effective expression
to Irish opinion, to study business and commercial relations
with a view to reconciling economic interests of North and
South and 'to bring home the fact that every effort to eradicate misunderstanding and disseminate good feeling in Ireland is a definite contribution to international peace and
security.'[12]

Although Charlemont remained a recognisable Unionist to
the end some of his liberal views were shared by the anti-populist wing of the Craig cabinet, ministers like Hugh Pollock
and James Milne Barbour, who opposed at times (but not
always) the populist sectarianism of the cabinet majority. The
one consistent anti-populist was Sir Wilfrid Spender, the head
of the Northern Ireland Civil Service, who logically enough
ended his days as an integrationist.[13] Montgomery, as these
texts show, began to question some of the most fundamental
premises of Unionism – essentially because he was keen to
secure Dublin's support in a war with Germany. His guiding
idea – perfectly understandable in the late 1930s – was that
Ireland should stand united with Britain against Hitler. It is all
the more important then to remember that Montgomery
remained a firm critic of the ethos of the south. He was, for
example, a patron of the often beleaguered Marie Stopes
Clinic in Belfast. In one remarkable passage General Montgomery publicly wrote:

The Ulster Plantation may have been an egregious blunder – I think it was – but it took place over three hundred years ago, and can no more be undone now than the Norman Conquest. It is not to be expected that the descendants of the Scottish and English planters of the 17th century will ever agree to be excluded from the British Empire. They have always been, and probably always will be, ready to fight rather than submit to anything of the sort; and people in the Free State will have to recognise this. . . .

I make bold to say that ninety per cent of us are decent, friendly, tolerant and patriotic people; and that, except in a few localities which I should prefer not to name, relations are, in ordinary times, perfectly amicable and neighbourly between the two sections in our community.

Further, I believe that if our leaders have the courage to put a case before us, where the choice lies between selfishness and self-sacrifice, we shall be ready to choose the latter, or at any rate to discuss its expediency, provided we are satisfied that the sacrifice *is* for the general good.

It must be clearly understood, however, that the sacrifice will *not* be made in order to bolster up a 'Republic', or a State which is not prepared to recognise the Crown as the connecting link between all the members of the Commonwealth.

Let us have a definite understanding with our friends across the border on these two points, and a realization on their part that concessions on our side must be met by reciprocal concessions on theirs. Of this realization there is at present, it must be admitted, very little sign.

It can be seen from this passage that Montgomery did not believe that the spirit of tolerance precluded some plain speaking. In 1938 an *ad hoc* group inspired by Montgomery prepared a leaflet setting out the aims of the proposed association. Briefly they were these:

to further better relations between

(a) Catholics and Protestants in Northern Ireland,

(b) the people of Northern Ireland and the Irish Free State,

(c) the people of Great Britain and Ireland.

This group had a number of members – notably Frank Reid, Brian Spiller, Cyril Nicholson, Mr and Mrs John Douglas, Miss Florence Greeves, Canon Brown, Rev Gerald Myles and Major G N Proctor. Soon the sympathies of eloquent (if marginal

politically) figures in the Irish Free State were engaged like
Donal O'Sullivan, Frank MacDermot[15] and J J Horgan[16], the
Redmondite contributor to the *Round Table*. MacDermot's lecture to the Belfast University Literary Society on 16 December 1936 summarised the views of this group. He insisted that
the attempt at Irish self-sufficiency was collapsing. He criticised Ulster's Unionists for their sense of superiority but
acknowledged that they had a right to resist efforts to break
their loyalty to the United Kingdom. Another member of this
group, George O'Brien, author of *Four Green Fields* (Dublin,
Talbot Press, 1937) was rather more Nationalist in tone;
O'Brien called for Irish judicial sovereignty over the whole
island but argued that 'corporate unity' was undesirable.
Despite clear differences of emphasis, these men agreed to
work together. Indeed, Montgomery even engaged the services of Sir Hubert Gough – best known for his part in the
'Curragh incident' in 1914 – and Limerick man Major-General Sir George Franks; these two served alongside Donal
O'Sullivan and John J Horgan as Vice-Presidents. In 1914
Gough had, in effect, been in Sir Edward Carson's camp while
Horgan had been firmly in Redmond's – at least this ancient
quarrel was buried. In more recent times, too, it is pleasant to
note that the Association's Council has been graced by representatives of families (Brugha and O'Higgins) who had suffered terribly as a result of the Irish civil war.[17]

Charlemont remained President for eight years; probably
only such a distinguished and aloof figure could have held the
Association together during the war (interestingly, the first
pamphlet of the Association – included here – deals very fairly
with the perception of the war as it existed in both parts of Ireland). Much to the frustration of the Southern members,
Montgomery tended to control access to Charlemont, who,
he explained, had largely taken on the office on condition
that he need only correspond with Montgomery![18] Eventually,
as Charlemont's health gave out, he handed over to the
thoughtful Trinity College, Dublin, academic Professor
Joseph Johnston who held office from 1946–1954. Johnston
was followed by the very successful Ulster businessman Sir
Graham Larmor (1897–1968) who held the presidency up to

1963. Larmor, a key figure in the Belfast business community, perhaps rather to his surprise, found himself embroiled in controversy with the Stormont government. In 1961, Sir Graham asked if the Irish Association membership could visit Government House, Hillsborough, as part of their annual conference programme. According to recently released Cabinet minutes: 'Prime Minister Lord Brookeborough said it would be a mistake to agree in view of the general background of the association and the fact that some of its objectives were suspect on political grounds.' There was clearly some dissent: 'It was pointed out that Sir Graham was a leading industrialist, trying to improve cross-border relations and trade and foster cultural and artistic contacts.' Nevertheless, Home Affairs Minister Brian Faulkner supported the Prime Minister. Faulkner said the association had commissioned an enquiry into the causes of tension in Northern Ireland. Its report was expected soon and 'would probably delve into allegations of intimidation, gerrymandering, discrimination in housing and similar topics, and display a strong anti-Unionist bias.'[19]

Throughout the 1960s, 1970s and 1980s there have been many significant interventions at Irish Association meetings. Prime Minister Terence O'Neill's address at a critical moment in his career convinced *Belfast Telegraph* editor, John Sayers, that his commitment to reform was more intellectual than emotional.[20] Cardinal Ó Fiaich gave a careful exposition of his views to the Association shortly after his elevation. In 1991, Unionist MP David Trimble provided a critique of the spirit of the Easter Rising of 1916. In 1992 Dr Conor Cruise O'Brien gave a typically forceful exposition of his views on the Northern question – a paper, which like many, provoked a lively debate amongst the membership. The important thing to note here is the range, quality and diversity of the contributors. This has been the hallmark of the Association throughout its life – an intense respect for diversity in an island which has often been fearful of a genuine pluralism. The letters[21] which follow were brought to the attention of the Association by Kenneth Darwin, then Director of the Public Record Office of Northern Ireland, in a lecture given on 16 April 1962. (We have re-edited these letters – in several cases providing a fuller text – but we have utilised his impeccable linking commentary which could hardly be improved upon.) The lecture was repeated for the Dublin branch of the Association and was attended by – amongst others – Conor Cruise O'Brien. It was reported in the *Irish Times* and Darwin shortly afterwards was reprimanded by Stormont Castle for associating with a 'subversive organisation'; an odd price to pay for outlining the thoughts of two members of the erstwhile Unionist establishment.

In a way, of course, the letters presented here are mainly examples of inter-Unionist dialogue rather than Unionist–Nationalist dialogue. In the course of these letters many caustic observations are made about mainstream Unionist politics in the 1930s. In case it should be thought that the governing party in the South was incapable of producing similar vigorous self-criticism, it should be pointed out that the correspondence of key figures in the Dublin governing party like Erskine Childers and Sean MacEntee was marked by an equally frank refusal of a pious self-serving tone. The University of Dundee's Richard Dunphy's excellent research is remarkable here.[22] Childers, for example, clearly feared that a Protestant was unlikely to be appointed as a Minister of Justice, Health, External Affairs, Education and probably Social Welfare or to local government appointments. MacEntee bluntly told DeValera: 'Why, we would not risk antagonising one Gaelic Leaguer or GAA crank in order to undo partition – as it could be undone tomorrow in sports and amusements'.[22] Naturally more robust spirits in Fianna Fail and the Unionist Party had no difficulty in dismissing the carping critics. George Bernard Shaw drew an unpalatable and possibly unfair conclusion in a letter to Sean O'Casey in 1950: Ireland having been the 'first flower of the earth' was now 'an insignificant cabbage garden . . . and our Fianna Fail Party is now the Unionist Party and doesn't know it'.[23]

One final comment may be in order. It is quite clear that the history of the Irish Association – despite its deep commitment to a better and more tolerant path – was not always marked by sweetness and light in its own affairs. Mary McNeill's

letters describe a bitter row between General Montgomery
and Donal O'Sullivan in 1942, with both men 'in a rage . . .
flying at each other'.[24] Eight years later, referring to another
Irish Association meeting, Mary McNeill wrote derisively
of 'these professional reconcilers', adding 'no one brings out
the devil of perversion in me to this extent . . . No, No,
No.'[25]

Two letters of hers reveal that tensions mark even the earliest days of the project. On 4 April 1938 Mary wrote to her
sister Peg:

Then there has been a complete standstill about General Montgomery's proposal. Mr Nicholson – the nice RC barrister, quite genuinely brought up an objection to the method and aims of the
proposed association and wanted people to meet to discuss them
further. General Montgomery, the apostle of reconciliations etc
etc etc, immediately took the huff – refused to meet Mr Nicholson
or discuss any of his points and wrote pages to him from Fivemiletown.

Meanwhile, quite a few of us met at Mr Nicholson's and discussed
his ideas. There was a very interesting RC lawyer there and really
one realised that he was talking about a set of people in Belfast completely foreign to the rest of us. The Brysons, Denis Ireland, John
Douglas and others were there, and the general opinion seems to
be against anything so official or critical as General Montgomery
was visualising. The General wants definitely to try to create contacts
between N & S, these others think that will be called political and
will be dangerous and they are on for creating better relationships
between Catholics and Protestants in Northern Ireland. As far as I
can see, I think the latter idea is too small and confined – I don't see
how you can go blethering to Catholics about goodwill if you are not
prepared to hold out some hope of fair treatment, and the minute
you touch that you touch the Northern government to the quick. I
think the General is right in theory, but he *will* insist on all sorts of
pomp and ceremony and vice-presidents and presidents of goodness
knows what, when it is something far smaller and more hand-picked
that is wanted. What is wanted is a collection of a few first class people on either side of the border to start evolving some kind of a policy and working along a variety of lines quietly before the whole thing
is broadcast about.

Then the General came to Belfast and I had him for an afternoon
and evening. I got John Douglas down in the evening to try to instill

into him the need for quiet work and they got on very well. John Douglas suggested a fascinating idea – instead of having a formal association why not have a bureau where all sorts of information on Irish affairs generally would be available and where there would be the machinery for getting research work done. It would be a sort of Institute of Ireland – it might arrange lectures, plan travel in Ireland – find out the real state of unemployment in Belfast and elsewhere, collect information that might be published in a sort of library, historical magazines, etc etc. It has possibilities – hasn't it?

To go at the political situation full steam ahead is almost impossible at present, but I am sure by a series of flank attacks the position can be made more and more ludicrous and unreal. A very interesting thing has happened just recently with an International Historical Society, in which countries are represented. Great Britain is represented and so is Eire but where was Northern Ireland to come in – they weren't getting any benefit from the English connection!! So it has been arranged – with the consent of the Eire government and the government of Northern Ireland – that on this association Ireland is to be represented as a *cultural whole*, sending two representatives, one to be from the National University and the other from either Trinity or Queen's. These are the kind of moves that are very important if worked in the right way.

The whole business of the Roman Catholic Church becomes more and more difficult to me. I think the Church as an organisation is a completely rotten affair (by the way what is happening about the Austrian cardinals?). I heard not long ago that it is becoming more and more impossible for lay Catholic teachers to get teaching jobs in the Free State because the Church is gradually getting all the schools into the hands of teaching orders – and why, because the lay teachers are so anti-clerical! (not anti-religious) and all this banning of books and preventing birth control clinics, etc etc is *rotten*. I sometimes think we are not ready for a settlement yet and before the final scheme will come there must be years and years of education and a purging of religion both Catholic and Protestant. The immediate solution is obviously some kind of a federal scheme like what G O'Brien suggests and if only the people with vested interests here in Northen Ireland, with their bleating about affection for an Empire, could be silenced I am sure it would be done without much trouble.

On 15 January 1939 she added:

Mind you, General Montgomery isn't the leader we want, it is to get the thing going and to be ready to pass on to someone else. I had got a bit discouraged about prospects till yesterday. I have people writing from all over the place saying how glad they are about this and what are we going to do? and no plan of action could I get General Montgomery to think about seriously. However, yesterday we went to Dublin merely to meet in a friendly way Mr Horgan who had come up from Cork. He is the RC and the chairman of the Bank Buildings!! The men all had lunch in a club and I went off to K Huggard, who, in the midst of collosal refugee work, mentioned a couple of men she had met who had recently come back from the Commonwealth Congress in Australia – a thing run by the Institute of International Affairs. One couldn't but be convinced that that was the type of person we wanted – not a whole bevy of retired British army generals. (It is an awful reflection on the Victorian backwardness of Northern Ireland that generals as generals do still cut ice on this side of the border – they certainly don't on the other!) At any rate I went down to the Hibernian Hotel where we were all to meet, and who do you think was sitting there with the General and Mr Horgan but Donal O'Sullivan, the most important of the two men K Huggard had mentioned. He is one of those marvellously educated RCs – Oxford and the Navy – Clerk in Mr Cosgrave's Senate, intimate friend apparently of Lionel Curtis etc etc. Mr Horgan also seems a good egg and altogether we had a very good afternoon's work. I feel if we can just get people like that to put their back into it, they won't want to see it flop.

These letters with their hint of social and feminist discontent give some idea of the difficulties of creating the Irish Association tradition. It is clear that those most committed to a non-sectarian path in Irish politics are often the most turbulent and non-conformist in spirit. Perhaps those of a most conformist mould are more easily drawn to the politics and practices of the main sectarian blocs? As a last word, the editors would like to point out that the views expressed here – by any of the correspondents – are not necessarily their own.

PART I

THE ORIGINS OF THE IRISH ASSOCIATION

1933–5
Early thoughts

In 1933 both Charlemont and Montgomery were alarmed by the growth of sectarianism in Ulster. The first important discussion came in a letter from Lord Charlemont to Montgomery on 14 April 1933 when they were discussing a particular case. Charlemont wrote:

Yes, it's a nasty business. Of course, anyone of our own class who does public work in this country is apt to come up against two things – (i) that the majority of the Protestants are really radicals although they belong to the Conservative party because it is Unionist[1], and (ii) that if he is a man of moderate views and has anything at all to do with Roman Catholics he is likely to get into trouble with the bigots of whom there are a great many. These are always with us but as a rule the bigotry is latent. At the present time, however, it is not so, and it must be admitted, I think, that this is due to the idiotic behaviour of the Roman Catholics themselves with their bonfires for DeValera. There is much the same sort of talk *here* because I employed a certain number of Roman Catholics on relief work. But I am not in any purely local politics and I am not an MP, so I only hear about it in a roundabout way. But when you are up against these two things *and* they are reinforced by the assistance of one class, undoubtedly it is a strong combination for one man to tackle. I am not sure that it is not the best thing to withdraw for the time being and to follow Montaigne's advice 'reculer pour mieux sauter'. The thieves may fall out or die or go away and one seldom loses anything by playing a waiting game.

A week later Lord Charlemont wrote again saying:

It's really rather a melancholy thing, perhaps even a little comic, to observe two male Partingtons considering how to combat the Catholic–Protestant complex! I fear it cannot be done; it is, I suppose, possible that it will have been swallowed up in other issues in another 300 years, but I'm not so darned certain. I am a Protestant and was born one, but I'm not a 'born Protestant'. I'm sure I would have been very happy as a Roman Catholic or a Hindoo, had my parents been of either persuasion.

There is a Protestant *temperament* – something to do with the ductless glands, I expect – and it is a physical fact as well as a state of mind. I think that blue eyes almost always go with it. But the major part of the Protestant population of Ireland is composed of these people. The point that I am getting at – for sooner or later I always get to the point – is that militant Protestantism is in their *blood* and no argument or reasoning power will get it out. They are, in fact, not responsible people in this direction and if they are low in class they can't restrain their actions either. If they see a trainful of RCs and there's a stone or two handy they must chuck it through a window. Mr Knox-Browne[2] (and many others in his class) would *like* to do this just as I would like to use bad language to deputations, but he is restrained by education and upbringing. My grandfather was a kindhearted man and deplored the fact that Roman Catholics were doomed to go to hell – it seemed rather unjust to him. But he never doubted that it *was* so. When you get a large proportion of gentry with these ideas, you cannot blame the peasants for acting on them. There are a certain number who do *not* agree, but hardly one of these likes to say what he thinks. Some because they lack the moral courage, some because they are lazy, some because they have an eye elsewhere. No one in any of the superior ranks of public life (myself, for instance) can say very much because they would embarrass the Government so horribly. Not that the latter are violent individually but they have to keep in with the Orange Order because it is a bulwark against Socialism. (Belfast would be largely Socialist tomorrow if it wasn't for the unswerving opposition to Socialism on the part of the Orange Order as a whole. I don't know that everyone knows this.) I do what little I can by employing some Roman Catholics – and it's an unpopular proceeding and I have had frequent complaint about it.

And the complainants have one form of argument that is a *good* one and which does not admit of a logical argument: 'In the bad times, would you have trusted any one of these Roman Catholics not to have burned your house down had he been told to?[3] If there were bad times again, would you trust any of them? Therefore why employ them? They would out you tomorrow if they had the chance.' I always reply: 'I was born and brought up under the British flag and under it all men are equal and must have a share in any employment that is going.' This doesn't admit of argument either – but it's not an answer to theirs.

I think there are two other reasons for this bitterness of feeling, both of them social ones.

(1) The large proportion of Roman Catholics in the population and the fact that they are increasing. People like ourselves often point out that there is very little anti-Catholic feeling in England or anti-Protestantism in the Free State. In both these countries the minority is so small that they do not matter – they can't exert much influence. There was plenty of religious bitterness in England in the sixteenth century when the sects were fairly evenly divided. The Roman Catholics are increasing here. I don't think there's much in the idea that they are coming in from the South. There may be a few instances, of course. I think, however, it's natural increase due to the virtual stoppage of emigration and the lower standard of life on the part of the Roman Catholics. It's like the Chinese in the FMS and South Seas. In another couple of generations the Protestant majority in Ulster will have vanished so far as I can see – and *then* there will be really jolly times which I am glad to think I will not see.

(2) The original Plantation settlers expelled all the better-class Roman Catholics, as they thought they might be a nucleus for rebellion. I daresay they were quite right, but it's a bad thing now from a political point of view as there are very few Roman Catholics who are really fit to take a good post. Where are my Roman Catholic Deputy-Lieutenants? I have *one* – but I wouldn't have had him had he been a Protestant. I think the

Government would have liked to have made a Roman Catholic judge when Megaw was made – but what Roman Catholic is the equal to Megaw? Not one. There are 20 Protestants or more who would have done. The best possible Roman Catholic was McGonigal[4] and he's a good advocate – but he hasn't the poise of a *judge*. We had the late Denis Henry and I have the present Bonaparte Wyse – both excellent but both Southerners.[5] Look at Devlin.[6] These people have *cunning* – but that's all.

In the lower posts – police and so on (Regan was a good C.I. – he comes from Clare) a proper proportion is kept, but you can't *get* the men for the better things. So the Roman Catholics *have* a grievance, but not one that can be redressed.

While I don't like the militant Protestants I don't like the Roman Catholics either, though I quite admit that the decent Roman Catholic is in rather a difficult position. But they are an ungrateful set – always complaining. You should hear their bishops talking about education where they get advantages unheard of in England. 'We are the underdog and must suffer' said T J Campbell KC[7] to me just after the Government had given the Roman Catholics a 50% grant for new schools – 50% out of public money and absolute ownership. He thought 100% would be the right thing. Then the stoning of pilgrims going to the Eucharistic Congress. Certainly a most deplorable thing but it only happened in three places that I know of; if you had read the *Irish News* you would have thought that every pilgrim got a black eye or a thick ear.[8]

Anyhow, all this doesn't make the life of the individual Minister any easier, and *I* am always balancing myself precariously on the tightest of ropes. I gave the Roman Catholic teachers a holiday to attend the Congress and was bombarded by Protestant societies about it. I composed a short reply to them of an extremely unpalatable nature which gave me great pleasure. Whenever I recognise a Roman Catholic school I am accused of being in the pay of the Vatican. The Roman Catholic hierarchy say that I am inspired by the blackest Protestantism. The Presbyterians say that I am Episcopal in all my appointments. The Church of Ireland say that my Parliamentary Secretary is a Presbyterian and regards education as a Presbyterian reserve. The Methodists say that they are never considered.

There are times when I would like to become a Hindoo, and
I certainly think that though it was bound to come, the Refor-
mation was one of the very greatest disasters that ever befell
humanity!'

To this letter Montgomery replied:

. . . I am quite sure there are large numbers of reasonable men
in Ulster who do not like the present state of things and I think
it altogether too pessimistic to regard oneself as a Mrs Part-
ington stemming the Atlantic with a mop. The principle of
tolerance has never really been fairly stated to the Protestant
population who are not in my experience deaf to argument.

*All through 1933–1934 and the first half of 1935 they continued
this correspondence on the relations of Protestants and Catholics in
the North in a series of similarly intriguing, forthright and enter-
taining letters. On 8 January 1934 Lord Charlemont wrote:*

We agree in the main, I think; I must necessarily make excuses
for the class to which I belong, but I do still believe that the
only chance the gentleman has of making his views known and
thus trying to get better and more moral views into the politician's head is to do it from inside the party. Otherwise we will
eventually get the same conditions that apply in municipal life;
the 'gentleman' criticises its obvious faults, but neglects the
only method by which he can make his criticism at all
constructive.

Of course the low status of the Roman Catholic population
in Ulster is due to the policy of the planters, but the Protestants can't well be blamed for what their remote ancestors did.
And I don't quite agree with Lord Clare; certainly Roman
Catholics are 'easily roused' but I do *not* think they are 'easily
appeased'. If England invented the Penal Laws she did
everything in her power to placate the Irish population from
the 'eighties on[9] – and has the result been any kind of
appeasement?

But, however all this may be, these people are *here*, and it
will cut matters short if I say that in general I am in agreement
with all you say.

Most of the harm, and the intense anti-Roman Catholic feeling has been, I think, the work of Ministers of Religion on both sides – the very people who should know better. I think, however, that the younger generations of Protestant clergy are more open-minded than their fathers or grandfathers, but it's the other way with the majority of young *priests.*

On 15 January 1935 Charlemont produced a memorandum on the question of Roman Catholic loyalty:

Can a Roman Catholic be loyal to a Protestant Government? Yes, I think so. As a class the English Roman Catholics were perfectly loyal to Queen Elizabeth's Government though it actually persecuted them. And also to Charles II's government under much the same conditions – they didn't have a good time when Titus Oates was about. Conversely many Protestants fought on the Roman Catholic side during the Thirty Years' War against the invading Swedes, and a large proportion of William's army at the Boyne were Roman Catholics – a fact forgotten by my Orange brethren. The thoughtful Roman Catholics in Ulster in these times will discount the exuberant utterances of politicians, even perhaps going so far as to allow for the circumstances in which they say them, for he knows that the ordinary Roman Catholic can go about his business without interference from anyone in the Administration. This wasn't the case in the United Kingdom under the Penal Laws but again Roman Catholics were perfectly loyal to the successive English Governments who administered these laws. It's far worse to live under oppressive laws than to have to read speeches in the *News Letter!*

1935–7
The riots of 1935: some strategic considerations

*In July 1935 there occurred a series of events in Belfast which gave
a serious point to their correspondence and that event was the Belfast
riots of that year in which several people lost their lives. It is probably
true to say that the Belfast riots[10] were really the events which created
in General Montgomery's mind the idea of the Irish Association. They
were certainly serious enough to make any person concerned about
relations between the two religious sections of the community take serious thought. In November 1933 the killing of a Catholic publican in
Belfast had marked the first sectarian murder in eleven years and in
1934 there had been isolated incidents of Protestant attacks on Catholic
homes in the city. By 1935, therefore, the celebration of George V's
jubilee by Protestants provided a potential spark for the increasing sectarian tension and the possibility of a major sectarian conflict, most
likely to occur on or around 12 July at the time of the Orange celebrations. With sectarian confrontations in May and June having led to
26 people being injured and more than 40 homes destroyed, the Minister of Home Affairs banned all parades from 18 June. Despite this,
when the Orange Grand Master (Sir Joseph Davison) warned that the
marches would go ahead anyway, the Stormont Government decided
to reverse its earlier decision and lift the ban. Nevertheless, as 'the
Twelfth' approached, tension grew.*

*On 2 July three people were wounded in Clifton Street when shots
were fired from North Queen Street as an Orange Procession marched
up Clifton Street after unfurling a new banner. None of the three men
wounded were in the Procession but were standing about at the street
corner. The same evening there was stone-throwing in Millfield and a
baton charge had to be made by the police after an attack on a Nationalist procession in Union Street. On 8 July the Church of Ireland Bishop
John MacNeice[11] made an appeal in a sermon in St Thomas's Belfast
and we quote this because this sermon obviously had the greatest*

influence on Montgomery's thought. The Bishop said: 'Wrong things are wrong whether they are done in Cork or in Belfast and wrong whether their authors are Roman Catholics or Protestants. But whether a man belongs to a majority or to a minority, society must protect itself against him if he proves himself lawless.' The Bishop went on to make an appeal for conciliation between both sides. On 11 July, the day before the main annual Orange marches, there was a debate at Stormont on the disturbances.

With tempers running high it took only a minor scuffle on the Twelfth between the Orange marchers and some Catholics to develop into a full scale riot, leading to 'the worst night of disorder since 1921–1922' according to the Northern Whig. *The* Irish News *reported: 'For over two hours battle raged between the opposing forces, and scenes that almost beggar description were enacted. Armoured cars, firing machine-guns, while police, armed with rifles or revolvers, fired upon gunmen and stone-throwers at all points, but from the corner of Donegall Street to the middle of York Street the fighting raged uninterruptedly for two hours.'*

The News-Letter *reported that two people had been killed on the Twelfth at seven o'clock in the evening as the main Orange Procession was returning from Belmont and 35 people were injured. There had been an attack at Stewart Street in the Markets area and then at North Street and at the junction of Donegall Street and York Street. On 13 July rioting had taken place before a curfew came into operation in the York Street area and two Protestants were shot. Sixty-one houses were attacked by mobs on Saturday and Sunday and the trouble spread to Sandy Row and Ormeau Road. On 15 July there was firing on the funeral of a Protestant in the York Street/Donegall Street area and reports started to appear of damage done in towns in the Free State, notably at Letterkenny in County Donegal. On 17 July 15 houses were set on fire in Belfast and a public appeal for peace was made by the Bishop of Down and the Dean of Belfast. On 18 July there was comparative peace as only eight houses had been set on fire.*

On 20 July the News-Letter *reported a joint meeting of ministers of the Church of Ireland, the Presbyterian and the Methodist Churches on the previous day at which a long resolution appealing for reconciliation and peace between all members of the community had been passed and the report of this meeting ended up with the following suggestive sentence 'Other suggestions were made in favour of the culti-*

*vation of goodwill and conciliation among all classes and creeds.' On
22 July the* News-Letter *reported another death, a bomb throwing
and riots in Limerick, Clones and several other places in the Free State.
By 25 July the* News-Letter *was able to headline 'Back to Normal'
but on 26 July it reported that the York Street Mill was closing because
of ill-feeling between the two religious groups of workers and 900 people would be unemployed. By 30 July Abyssinia was the main news
headline. In the end, eight Protestants and five Catholics were killed.
One commentator has concluded: 'There had been more deaths in the
Protestant community but Catholics had suffered most in other respects.
The great majority of the wounded were Catholic; over 2,000 Catholics
and only a handful of Protestants were driven from their homes; and
95% of the 21,699 compensation for destruction to property was paid
out to Catholics.'[12]*

*It was at this time that Montgomery seems first to have suggested
to Lord Charlemont the idea of some organisation like the Irish Association. Charlemont in typical manner referred to it as the ABC and
in a letter of 14 August 1935 he discussed his objections to such an
organisation and his being in favour of organising a deputation to
the Prime Minister instead. He wrote:*

You have, as you know, my complete sympathy but I do *not*
approve of your idea – at any rate, not *in toto*. I think there is
something to be said for it in Local Government elections but
grave objections in parliamentary *ditto* and I am not sure that,
in practice, it would be possible to separate the one from the
other.

*It would appear that Montgomery was suggesting the formation of
a group of people to form a third party or independent pressure group
between the Unionists and the Nationalists. Charlemont continued:*

The ABC would attract to itself a great many cranks who have
their own differences with the Government as it is; they would
render lip service to the ABC, of course. Even if this didn't
happen, the ABC would only count as one more party of independent Unionists – you would be in with the Nixons[13] and
Hendersons[14]. No, from a political point of view I think it would
be dangerous as it would tend to split the party. Politicians are
also like every other kind of professional men – they look at

everything from a political point of view, their own view, that is – and you and those who acted like you would destroy the very influence you hoped to exert by being classed with the ex-moderator and *his* crew, Redmond the Fruit-man and *his*, and so on.[15] You can, of course, discount all this by saying: 'Of course, Charlemont is a politician and looks on this as he admits politicians do and he thus destroys his own argument.' However this may be it is my view.

And yet I don't like to dismiss the notion entirely; I do think there is quite a large body of public opinion with you; maybe a good deal larger than you think and I believe it includes a very influential body of men – or many of them – amongst *Traders*. I know one at least who feels very strongly on the subject.

Now I do not think that any society in the world could stop the Murphys[16] and the Dean Kings;[17] the thing is in their blood and the thing that makes the fanatic is that he cannot listen to reason – the Ethiopian cannot change his skin or the leopard his spots. But it's possible to influence the Government and I am a great believer in deputations *if* the particular deputation is an influential one. Of course it all depends on personnel – every human activity does when you come to think of it. Now, whatever may be said against the Government I don't think anyone can say (with justice) that it is unapproachable, and I think that were you to take a little time and gather together such a deputation to the Prime Minister it would have a good effect, for you must remember that there are certain members of the Government who are sympathetic. I don't think that in the past the latter have been sufficiently outspoken in their opinions; it is agreeable to be in a Cabinet, the members of which are all friends, but it has its drawbacks from the point of view of public policy. I wish the moderates had taken a stronger line after Basil Brooke's Derry speech,[18] but they said to themselves: 'We didn't know he was going to say this, it is said now and we cannot unsay it; Basil will be a good Minister of Agriculture and we do not want to be unkind to him just as he is starting and he will learn more sense as he goes on' and (from his last speech) I think he *has*.

Now I have done something – I have offered you an alternative policy to which you can at least give a *trial.* You cannot do a thing like this all in a minute, the thing will take time.

Having got your deputation, you could say to the Prime Minister: 'We are representing this to you for your own good for we have the same political ideals as you have – we only think you are not in the way to attaining them with these methods of absolute cleavage between two-thirds of the population to the other third. If you agree, well and good; if you persist in your own view, we are against you'.

Now, I don't know whether you know the 'Belfast Businessman'. He has much more common sense in political affairs than is often thought. I would like you to have a talk with Captain Dashwood[19] of Messrs Coates Ltd, Belfast. He *is* Coates Ltd. As he told me he had lost a lot of contracts from Basil's Derry speech. I am certain he would agree with you and he would know better than I do who you can count upon in the business world in Belfast. Money talks, you know; it has always done so.

Having talked to Dashwood, you would pick your deputation with the greatest care, taking pains to eliminate from it anyone who anyone could call a crank. My reason for wishing to include businessmen is that they are seldom cranks and as they seldom intrude in politics though their support is all-important to a Government their views are likely to be listened to with respect. But I don't wish to exclude the best type of country gentleman; he is influential too if he only has the courage of his opinions. Without that – in my opinion – he is NBG to anyone!

Montgomery appears to have had doubts about the wisdom of Charlemont's suggestion and to have suggested that such a deputation might get plausible replies and no more. On 18 August Charlemont replied:

. . . But a *strong* deputation will be able to make itself impressive, and convey the idea that present words without future deeds will not be altogether satisfactory to either party. But even if a deputation accomplishes nothing in itself it will draw 'your party' together and show you who can be counted on, for (as I said before) people who have not got the courage of their convictions are no good to you or anyone else. Yes, I think it would be an excellent thing to include a Free Stater if he was a good representative of his class.

Even knowing him as well as I do I don't know really whether the Prime Minister inclines to your views or Basil's – although I know *Lady* Craigavon's views perfectly well![20] Lord Craigavon is far more emotional than you would think and, among his own people, he is sometimes led to say things like 'A Protestant Government for a Protestant people' which I am sure he regrets afterwards. Also his immediate entourage is intransigent and although I am sure he knows Burke's 'The Whole Art of Politics is to hear not those who speak but those who are silent', the silence of those who feel as you do has been so intense that it would have required more the ear of the weasel to hear them than the ear of a human being! And in response to any gesture to the Roman Catholics, any inkling of the possibility of an appointment, the ears of Ministers are *deafened* by screams – 'You don't know what it is like' 'Everything in Northern Ireland (in education) is showered on the Roman Catholics, may not we Protestants have at least a share in these benefits', wrote the Dean of Derry to me a week or two ago. And he's not alone – there is lots like him. No, one can certainly blame the Prime Minister, but there is a lot of excuses for him. I don't know that it would not be a good thing if you had a personal interview with him to start with – but MacNeice is the first man to consult.

Three weeks later Charlemont seemed to have changed his mind somewhat about the deputation proposal and advised a patient and long-term campaign to Montgomery. On 3 September he wrote as follows:

The Deputation idea was *only* an idea, but even were it a good one the time is not nearly ripe for it. You have, in fact, to get your ABC before you can start on the D! Or, as you are a soldier and (in Great Britain anyhow) civilians have always told soldiers how to conduct campaigns, in order to do so you have first to get your troops and munitions, then to formulate your strategy and then to decide where the best chances of attack lie; after that you will explain to your commanders how it's to be done and (perhaps) listen to what they say. Then you do it and continue to do it.

At the present moment you haven't got any troops and you don't know where to attack either for there's no very suitable ground for you, even if you had an army. Obviously you can't attack a Government for what one of its members said a year ago – and is probably sorry for. You're not even quite sure that the Government is an enemy at all! If they're not, well and good. If they are, you must wait until they do something which will give you a chance – or say something.

You will be able to judge their general attitude better when Parliament meets, which it will do early in October.

But, in my opinion, it's all important for the ABC *never* under any circumstances whatever to join up with any political party; for if the ABC failed in their first engagements (which is quite likely seeing what they are up against) it would stultify the whole movement if they joined the 'Back to Westminster' party – a party that is pre-doomed to failure as Westminster wouldn't have them back at any price. If, at a future time, the ABC were forced to threaten action, or to take it, it would be *in*action, 'non-co-operation', a very serious attitude for any body of Unionists to take up and the more so because it is invulnerable. But, at the nearest, any action of that kind is two years or so away.

The Country Gentleman is in a rather difficult position in this matter, for he is either in politics when he is on the Government side, or he isn't, and then he has only a limited amount of weight to throw about. And also he isn't numerous as a class in this country. One naturally thinks of one's own class first, but your best troops will be found in the business community. The one in Belfast is going to have to put its hands in its pockets to *pay* for all the fun in that city, and though a financial grievance may not be so spiritually high as a moral one I am not at all sure that it hasn't more driving power! The very fact that the average business man desires to keep out of ordinary politics would make him more amenable to your ideas. I shall be interested to hear what the Bishop of Down thinks, and I think the Primate might be consulted also; he is a very far-sighted politician. But there's nothing to be gained by hurrying; the ABC is out to combat a state of mind which has existed for a very long time and it would be better worthwhile to spend six months on getting hold of one or two *good* men than to rush into deputations and the like with 'go-getters'!

About 20 August, however, Montgomery seems to have thought the idea of a society to spread a spirit of mutual tolerance in Northern Ireland was worthwhile for he appears to have written to a very representative cross section of the community enclosing a reprint of the Bishop of Down's, that is, Bishop MacNeice's sermon on conciliation and some other enclosures of a similar nature. The replies which he received are extremely interesting and give an idea of the opinion of his fellow-countryman at that time. They are a good deal more informative and interesting than letters on this topic which were appearing in the News-Letter *at the same time and Montgomery himself did not take part in newspaper correspondence until 19 September which was almost a month after he had issued his series of private letters to individuals suggesting some organisation.*

The following extracts from representative groups such as academics, landlords, ministers of religion, optimists and pessimists give a revealing insight into the attitudes of different groups at that time. Robert W Bingham, a Dungannon headmaster, wrote on 24 August:

I am heartily in sympathy with any movement which will tend to spread a spirit of mutual tolerance in Northern Ireland and I think there is at the present time a general tendency even among members of the Government to foster the growth of such a spirit. I believe that a good deal of good would be done by the distribution of literature such as you have sent me and the numerous quiet discussions which it would provoke. I do not think, however, that the formation of anything of the nature of an Association would be a wise step. . . . The Association would provide a definite target for attack and misrepresentation by opponents and perhaps become a symbol of lukewarm Protestantism to bigoted diehards.

. . . Bigotry and intolerance are not rampant throughout Northern Ireland. The great mass of the people are large hearted and tolerant and would welcome such a movement. The bigoted and intolerant are much more noisy and outspoken but there is no sign of this antagonistic feeling among ordinary people in their daily intercourse. Outside politicians and clergymen, men of standing do not make inflammatory speeches. There are the few exceptions; these are only (a) members of old families who are following family traditions and lack the courage or initiative to break with it and (b) place seekers keeping 'in the limelight'. The politicians and class (b) will follow the trend of expressed public opinion, class (a) and the militant clergymen will in the end follow the leads of the heads of their respective churches and many would be influenced by the distribution of this literature.... The Twelfth of July is a day when a great deal of harm is done. Certain politicians and clergymen seem to think that they have a licence to make speeches on that day which are antagonistic to all they preach during the remainder of the year. This day, however, is the one great holiday of the year for a great mass of the people in the country districts. They have no views on the spending of it beyond going to 'The Field'. If it were possible by the arranging of an increased number of general excursions to spread the view that this day is a general holiday of the August Bank Holiday type many of the younger generation would be saved from a great deal that is harmful.

The same person writing a week later stated that he did not think that a deputation to the Prime Minister would be helpful until later on when a more considerable body of people had been stirred to activity. He thought such a deputation would, at that time, be graciously received, listened to and given a soothing reply and that nothing would be achieved. He continued:

With regard to finding a nucleus in each district. It will only be possible to start slowly. . . . Personally, I would be glad to do what I could among the heads of the various schools in Northern Ireland and I feel sure that quite a number of them would sympathise and probably be helpful.

In University circles where one might have expected strong support for Montgomery's views he met a disappointing attitude. Professor R M Henry[21] wrote (17 September 1935):

Thank you for your letter and for the cutting from the newspaper and the re-print of the Bishop's sermon on conciliation which you enclosed.

I am heartily in favour of something being done to further

the object which you and the Bishop alike have at heart, but I am a little in doubt as to the best way in which that can be promoted. To have a definite movement in the sense of a public Manifesto or Committee might, I think, cause misconception as if the object were more or less political. It seems to me that there is much to be said for the view that in the present state of feeling and until excitement has died down, it is better to use one's private influence as widely as possible and not start a public movement.

I spoke to several people who I thought might join such a movement if it were started and I think that all of them while sympathetic gave me various reasons why it would be better that they should not take any public part; so while I am entirely in favour of the object you have in view I am a little doubtful as to the proper method of approach.

One of those to whom Montgomery wrote was John Andrews,[22] then the Minister of Labour at Stormont and later Prime Minister. A letter of 3 September said:

I read your speech at Comber in yesterday's papers with great interest and was very glad to see you laying it down that 'civil and religious liberty for all' includes 'our opponents as well as ourselves, provided they act constitutionally and keep within the laws of the land'.

But I hope you will forgive my saying that I was surprised at the second paragraph, in which it was implied that this was a recognised attitude of long standing on the part of the Government, which had met with no response from our Roman Catholic opponents.

My recollection is that the last official reference to the subject was on the occasion when you and your colleagues were publicly identified by the Prime Minister, in Parliament (20 March 1934) with Basil Brooke's remarks at Derry on the previous day, when he accused '99%' of our Ulster Roman Catholics of being disloyal without producing one vestige of evidence, in law or otherwise, and advised Protestants not to employ them.

Knowing your normally tolerant views, it seems to me very unlikely that you were consulted by the Prime Minister before this rash statement was made. But, as it has never been withdrawn or repudiated, Roman Catholics can hardly be expected to realise this; especially when the statement was followed up later in the year by the Prime Minister's further dictum about 'a Protestant Government for a Protestant people', which has been so widely quoted by our own extremists as well as by the other side.

Incidentally, Mr Reid, who followed you at Comber, seems to have quite misunderstood the ... objections to that remark: There is little to find fault with in the expression 'a Protestant Government', which is a mere statement of fact when all the members of the Cabinet are Protestants; but to use the words 'for a Protestant People' when referring to a population one third of whom are Papists, is surely to incite to disloyalty every self-respecting Roman Catholic in the six counties.

After reading this, and some of the speeches to which we have been treated by Davison[23], Murphy, Grant[24] and others, I confess I was not at all surprised to see the statement in the *Manchester Guardian* to the effect that 'the Catholics have been taught to regard themselves as natural enemies of the state, and they can hardly be blamed if they have taken the lesson to heart'; or at the reproof administered by the Belfast Coroner to 'so-called leaders of public opinion'.

Now, my object in writing this is not to find fault, but to ask whether, having laid down the very solid proposition referred to at the beginning of my letter, you would not consider going one step further and supporting a movement, which some of us are thinking of starting, to ensure that Roman Catholics who *do* act constitutionally and keep within the bounds of the law shall be treated with greater courtesy and consideration than they have been up to now.

Such a movement need be in no sense 'against the Government', and might even be useful in strengthening its hands when dealing with the Briscoes and Nixons. It would of course be in favour of suppressing the IRA and anyone who adopted *un*-constitutional methods.

John Andrews replied to Montgomery's letter on 8 September 1935:

I am gratified that you approved of what I said a few days ago. I simply expressed the views I have always held in this connection. You will appreciate that it is sometimes difficult to play the team game. As a member of the Government I don't think it would be possible to join the society to which you refer. The great difficulty in Ulster is, of course, that so many Roman Catholics are disloyal and determined to continue to work to put us in the Free State.

The correspondence between Montgomery and Andrews continued for the rest of the year with the two generally agreeing to disagree. On 30 October Andrews wrote:

Dear General

In reply to your kind letter, I quite admit that the position is extremely difficult. It is almost impossible, I fear, to cultivate a feeling of goodwill in Ireland between the different parties. It is true that some of the representatives of the Nationalist Party are reasonably moderate, but some of them, on the other hand, are just as extreme as the Republicans and are also working for a United Irish Republic.

A speech such as that delivered by Mr John D Nugent [a former Nationalist MP and leading Hibernian] and reported in the *Irish News* today, and also the one published by Bishop Mageean [Bishop of Down and Connor] a few days ago, is what aggravates our people.

Frankly, I fear until the demand for a 'United Irish Republic' is dropped by our opponents, there will be no peace and goodwill.

On 6 November another letter from Andrews added that:

The reasoning of these Republican candidates is not helpful towards a new spirit! They will, at any rate, show how many downright disloyalists exist in the parts of our area where they are standing for election.

The attitude of the landlords and country gentry varied greatly. The following letter from Brigadier H G Young[25] on 28 August is perhaps typical of the sympathetically pessimistic writers:

I have read your letter with interest and I entirely agree in principle with everything you say and you have my entire sympathy. *But* I am afraid it is a hopeless task to try and alter the

present situation. There are two main reasons in my mind for
the present state of affairs – first, the Orange Order (which
incidentally I loathe) where unfortunately the tail wags the
dog. No Unionist politician dare say anything against them or
their excesses or he would lose his seat. The only politician
I know who might assist you in any way is Colonel Alec
Gordon.[26]

He, being a soldier, holds much the same views as you and
I do and I know he is not an Orangeman. The second reason
for the present situation is the behaviour of the Nationalist
Members who, although personally on good terms with members of the Government and often getting favours from them,
never cease in their speeches vilifying them – for propaganda
purposes they will never admit that the Government does anything good and always attribute the lowest motives to them.

In your campaign you might possibly get a few Protestants
of standing to support you – perhaps a good number: but I
am afraid your difficulty will be to get one Catholic to support
you. So far as I know there is not one single Catholic who would
take an individual and patriotic line. As far as I am concerned
– as you know I am the Serjeant at Arms and a Civil Servant
and thereby debarred from taking any part in politics and you
cannot separate this movement entirely from politics. Now for
practical proposals. I believe you can do nothing unless you
get a hold of a few influential Roman Catholics – if you could
get a few such I would suggest your sending Lords Bangor,[27]
Dunleath[28] and Kilmorey.[29] I am sure they would be in sympathy and would form a nucleus but without the Papishes they
can do nothing.

If you get such a quorum I believe an appeal in the papers
signed by them and asking for support might have some
effect. . . .

*Montgomery did, in fact, have letters from both the Colonel and the
peers mentioned in this letter. Dunleath wrote a letter which made a
somewhat unlikely proposal but which was probably perfectly sincere.
Dunleath wrote (10 Sept. 1935):*

I am afraid I have been a long time answering your letter of
29 August, but it arrived when I was in Scotland, and since I

have returned I have had a large accumulation of work to go through, and am only now beginning to get clear of it.

I do not think there are any educated people in Northern Ireland who would not wish to support a movement in favour of more tolerance; and who, I think, would not be agreed that some steps should be taken.

The only debatable point, which appears to me, is what method should be employed? I, personally, do not consider that a movement outside the existing organisations would do much good; there is no doubt that, for the moment, a new movement might work, but I do not think it would have any lasting results.

I have been thinking over your letter for the last few days and I think that if we are really to do any good it should be done through the Orange Institution. One of the main points in the Orange Institution is that its members should abstain from all uncharitable thoughts, words or actions towards their Roman Catholic brethren, and this point might very well be emphasised, if you could get in touch with the leaders of the Orange Institution and talk it over with them. I am quite sure that this would be infinitely the best way of creating a more tolerant feeling and it might be possible to include a resolution, appealing for tolerance, to be passed on the next Twelfth July.

If you work through the existing Orange Institution you will reach practically every Protestant in Northern Ireland, either directly, or indirectly, whether educated or uneducated, whereas the intolerance exists chiefly amongst those who have little or no education.

On 26 September Lord Kilmorey replied:

I do not take any active part in politics – but at the same time I quite agree with the statements and sentiments expressed by our leading North of Ireland statesmen – [I] only wish that both parties would try and work together for the common good of all men.

I fear this Utopian situation is hardly likely to take place either in this island or on the continent.

Colonel Gordon (13 September) commented on Dunleath's proposal as follows:

I do not think Lord Dunleath's proposal to work through the Orange Order is practical: at least for those who do not belong to it: the obvious answer 'You should join the Order if you want to influence public opinion through it.' The present leaders are and have been committed to anything but moderate action and opinions. If Dunleath can get them to have more tolerant resolutions next year, well and good, he can try and if successful it would certainly do good.

I would certainly say a private meeting to talk things over would be good. A public meeting at present, no: the Protestant League would bust it up: also Glengall Street [Unionist Party Headquarters] would say we were a lot of traitors!!

I have spoken to one or two people in various grades of society; the higher you go the more you are likely to get a rebuff. The Prime Minister is to speak at a public meeting on 17 October in Downpatrick and I will try and speak to him before it so as to see if he can put a check on these extreme views of religious hatred: . . .

On the morning after this meeting the Northern Whig *reported:*

A stirring appeal to the Loyalists of Northern Ireland to remain united against their enemies was made by Viscount Craigavon, Prime Minister, at a Unionist demonstration in Downpatrick last night.

He pointed out that if there was any division in their ranks as a result of too many Protestant organisations Ulster might find itself voted into the Free State. Once there it would be impossible to get free. Lord Craigavon denounced the 'poisonous stories which have been let loose against Ulster'. 'We will take steps,' he said, 'to counteract these calumnies and the vituperation of the Nationalist Press'.

Lord Craigavon said it was almost 30 years since they had first met together in the same hall. During that period they had gone through crisis after crisis, but had pulled through on every occasion.

Great changes had taken place. His colleagues and himself

had taken up the reins of Government. They had done their utmost to lift up Ulster, not to keep her back, and certainly not to allow her to take a retrograde step.

He paid tribute to Sir Basil Brooke, who had done his best to get for Ulster all the advantages that could be got from close association with the great British market.

In reply to a question by the Prime Minister as to whether they would again offer their services to the County Down electorate at the general election for the Imperial Parliament Lord Castlereagh and Mr D D Reid replied in the affirmative.

Turning to the audience he asked them if they wanted their present members to be returned. The question was greeted with a burst of cheering and cries of 'Yes'. Referring to Colonel Gordon the Prime Minister said that during his time in the House he had found him to be a true friend, especially of the agricultural community in the area.

Continuing, he said that three questions engaged the minds of the public at the moment.

On an Orange platform in South Armagh recently he ventured to point out that they in Ulster could not afford to have too many organisations. They had the Orange, the Black, the Apprentice Boys, and the various Unionist associations, and the reason why he mentioned the subject was this. He referred to the start of the Scottish Protestant League and quoted an article from its official organ, which was to the effect that –

'Had not the Scottish Protestant League put candidates up in various wards there would still be a Moderate majority in Glasgow Town Council.'

He mentioned this because in a town council like Glasgow if seats were lost they could be won again. If, on the other hand, too many seats were lost in Ulster, and Ulster was voted into the Free State, they could not recover from the position.

If such a thing happened it would not matter what the feelings of regret were. It would not matter the heart burnings.

'If you take the wrong turning,' he said, 'and let yourself be thrown into the Free State you cannot vote yourself out once you are in'.

He appealed to those likely to drift to stand firm as their forefathers had stood and not to break the ranks.

In a reference to the Social Credit System he said the scheme
was being tried out in Alberta, Canada, and he appealed to
the people of Ulster not to burn their fingers but to wait and
see how it worked out there. They would learn by the experience of Alberta.

When it had been proved a success then it was time to take
it up, and the people of Ulster would find that the Northern
Government was never behind any other Government.

Speaking of the critics of the Northern Government the
Prime Minister appealed to the people of Ulster not to place
too much faith in the 'whispers' which were going round about
the Northern Government. These were exaggerated as they
went on. He would rather that the people who 'whispered' so
unfairly would come to him, or would ask Colonel Gordon to
ask a question on the floor of the House. He (the Prime Minister) would answer any question truthfully as to exactly how
matters stood. If people were only more open and frank there
would be far less unrest among a certain section of their
people.

They had opponents in England and Wales who would like
to see them crushed out. They had their critics in the Press,
whose stories were poison let loose and whose desire was to
throw them into the Free State.

'We will take steps to counteract these calumnies and vituperation of the Nationalist Press, and we ask you to present a
united and solid front at all times, but especially in difficult
times.'

Viscount Castlereagh, MP, in a reference to the Ulster Government, said that although the province was young it was
being efficiently governed. They must stand behind the Prime
Minister, however, to preserve their liberties and their vital
connection with Britain. . . .

Lieutenant-Colonel Gordon, MP, said that those who criticised the Ulster Government should think once, twice, and
for a long time before doing anything to undermine the Constitution which made Ulster a part of the United Kingdom.

Mr D D Reid, chairman of the Ulster Unionist Party at Westminster, said that the decision of the National Government to
have a General Election was wise. They were at the beginning

of a difficult situation, and it was necessary that a Government should be the mouthpiece of the people of the United Kingdom.

The manifesto which the Unionist Party at Westminster issued about the July riots in Belfast was following on one by the Nationalists. If a Nationalist manifesto such as had been issued had been read in a hall like that it could be blown to pieces.

When 'facts' were torn from the circumstances from which they had arisen they looked extremely discreditable.

That was the sort of thing that the Unionists at Westminster had to face every week and every month, and it was their duty to explain to representatives of cross-channel constituencies the truth of the situation.[30]

On 27 October the Colonel wrote again:

... You will have seen that the Prime Minister practically said nothing in his speech and covered a lot of ground. I was not reported in the press but told the meeting that the minority were just as entitled to civil and religious liberty as they were and that I would support the Government in seeing that there was no persecution of Roman Catholics because of their religion.

Many people of all ranks of society and amongst the decent class of Orangeman have since thanked me for what I said but it certainly did not please the type that supports the Protestant Leaguers. However, if decent people, and particularly the younger generation, continue to use their influence for peace and in time with the influence of the Church a better feeling is bound to come. If at the coming election the Republicans put up candidates there will be a lot of hard things said and feeling aroused but one can only go on quietly doing what is right.

From the landed gentry outside active politics there was a good deal of support and the following letter from Capt H K Dobbs[31] (26 August 1935) expresses their views:

More power to your elbow! I have been hoping for years that some day someone of position and influence would come forward and preach the gospel of tolerance and mutual goodwill.

If there is anything I can do to help you in an advance, however small, towards the ideals suggested in your letter, you can count on me to the limit of my ability. Now for a few remarks on the subject.

1 I am firmly convinced that there is an extraordinarily large body of enlightened opinion only waiting for a lead in the direction to which you point.

2 This body of opinion has so far been almost inarticulate owing to – (a) the general lethargy which is such a common failing of humanity, (b) the absence of any active nucleus round which to form and from which the necessary force could be derived to overcome the *dio inertiae*.

3 The greatest difficulty I foresee in attaining tangible results comes from two radically opposed sources:

(a) the intransigent and mutual admiration cabal known as 'The Government of Northern Ireland'.

(b) the Roman Catholic hierarchy and the Nationalist leaders.

The former (and their supporters) regard anyone who dares to criticise them and their methods as beyond the pale, and unfortunately this body includes all those so justly and strongly indicted by the Coroner in the remarks you enclose.

The latter, under the baleful influence of Cardinal Macrory[32] would be, I fear, very difficult to conciliate, and just as it takes two to make a quarrel it likewise takes two to come to an agreement!

At the same time, there is no achievement without effort and the aim is high – so, in God's name, go forward and good luck to you.

I will do anything I can to help and do not think I would have any difficulty in getting a decent body of influential assistance in this part of the Six Counties.

Festina lente should certainly be our motto – let me know how you propose getting the movement under way – do you think of trying to rope in representatives of *all* classes from the very beginning? The idea is big in every way.

There was, of course, a good deal of strong opposition, some of it more moderate than the rest. Viscount Bangor (September) wrote as follows on this theme:

. . . I need hardly say that I am all in favour of toleration. I live in a very Roman Catholic district and we all get on very well together but in my opinion the priests are the trouble and I am convinced that they instil hatred of everything to do with Great Britain and instead of the children of both dominations growing up together as friends the whole object of the priests appears to be in the other direction. I can give you an instance. There was a school here where there was about two thirds Roman Catholics to one third Protestant under lay management. This scheme had been going on for a 100 years and the children were all good friends. The manager decided to transfer the school and what was the result? The priest took every Roman Catholic child away and was allowed by the Government to establish a school of his own less than a quarter of a mile away where there was ample accommodation for everybody. This also of course means four teachers where two could be sufficient. I have a school of my own of which I am manager. There are about 90 on the rolls and about two thirds are Roman Catholics. The assistant teacher is always Roman Catholic and the children get on first-rate. Fortunately I have an endowment which helps to run the school. Suppose I were to transfer it, what would be the result? Just the same as the other school. For the moment it does not suit the priest to take away the children. I have come to the conclusion that the Roman Catholics are impossible. They are always *whining* over the harsh treatment which they receive whereas I think that they are treated very fairly. I am always listening to this in the Senate. . . . I cannot believe that many of them are loyal. They certainly do not try to meet us in any way and I am afraid that I should not be inclined to trust many of them.

I think a great deal of harm is done by writing inflammatory letters to the press but I do not think that any movement in the direction in which you suggest would be of much use. I think the Roman Catholics led by their priests would only laugh at it. We have always got on here quite harmoniously and I have people coming up here if they want anything quite irrespective of creed. Still, I firmly believe that the whole cause of the troubles in Ireland are due to religion. Everybody is entitled to his religious convictions and I am all for liberty of conscience but I have a horror of the methods of the Roman Catholic Church and though individually we can be friendly I cannot imagine really friendly relations existing between the two parties. I wish I could but as I said before the priests are the obstacle.

A more direct disagreement, but courteously phrased, came from a neighbouring landlord and family friend, Basil Brooke, on Boxing Day 1935:

I am afraid your letter and mine in reply show the futility of discussing such matters by assertions on one side and disclaimers on the other. I admit that you suggested that I should not reply but if I do not you are liable to take it that I agree by default.

We can but agree to differ and I can only repeat that I have no animosity against any man whatever his religion. But I will do all I can to prevent disloyalists from including Ulster in the Free State and smashing our Constitution.

Montgomery continued to write an annual letter to Brooke deploring his Twelfth speeches. Meanwhile, the sounding out of opinion continued. The Reverend Professor Corkey,[33] a prominent Presbyterian, disapproved of any action such as Montgomery suggested and gave the following reasons on 4 September 1935:

I fully sympathise with your desire for the creation of a spirit of goodwill between the Protestant and Roman Catholic sections of our community in Northern Ireland and I agree with you that more might be done for the cultivation of such a better spirit.

I think, however, that at the present time great care would have to be taken in initiating a movement for this end. It would be quite unfair, I think, and possibly only harmful to do or say anything that would seem to suggest that the Protestant people or their orators were primarily responsible for the recent disturbances in Belfast. The Protestants indeed and their leaders are not without some responsibility but, so far as my judgement goes, the trouble was started by angry mobs of Nationalists. You will, I know, not misunderstand me when I say this. The Roman Catholic people were roused to a great pitch of irritation by the Jubilee celebrations. I witnessed small but vicious manifestations of this irritation at that time myself.

That irritation had not subsided when the Twelfth July demonstration came along and it almost inevitably gave fresh vent to itself at that time.

I agree, however, with you that more could and should be done amongst our Protestant people to avoid disgraceful repetitions of the recent disturbances. I think positive action might safely be taken along two lines. First, an effort might be made to impress upon all Protestant 'orators' the importance of urging in all their utterances the duty of kindliness and goodwill towards their Roman Catholic neighbours while at the same time maintaining in every legal way their present rights. Second, I think that these 'orators' and all Protestant leaders should be prompted to impress upon their people the iniquity and utter folly of sporadic retaliation whenever any provocation is given. The Protestant mob in Belfast has seriously damaged Ulster's prestige in the eyes of the world by their recent criminal efforts to get their own back. I feel that we Protestant people can safely rely on our police force and our Government to mete out all the retribution on evil doers that is needed for the maintenance of our security. That, I think, should be soundly impressed upon every Protestant and if that were done one of the prime conditions of these occasional disturbances would disappear.

So far as the inculcation of these two elementary duties upon the minds of our more thoughtless people is concerned you can count on me to give whatever support I can. I think we could do with a great deal less public political demonstration but I am afraid it would be hopeless to propose anything of this sort at the present time.

Everybody, however, was not as moderate as this. A local country gentleman, Colonel John McClintock[34] on 2 March 1935 wrote:

I cannot understand why you are occasionally pleading with Ulster to give half an inch to the Free State. All we in Ulster want is to stick to the British Empire and be under the King. We are Loyalists and do not want to be under DeValera. You, I expect, are a Loyalist and it does seem so odd to give in in any way. Why not write to the Irish papers and suggest to them that they should unite with us in being loyal to the King and Empire – that would be the only sort of united Ireland we can contemplate but do not ask us to repudiate our loyalty to an Irish Republic.

Another country gentleman, Sir Charles Langham,[35] *wrote on 31 August:*

If you had asked me 25 years ago I should have quite agreed with you but my eyes have been opened since then and I really now quite understand the animosity which I never did in the old days. I won't say more in a letter. . . .

A great many of the letters which Montgomery received misunderstood his appeal and are evidence in themselves of the necessity for his appeal. Essentially he was appealing for mutual tolerance. A great many people seem to have assumed that he was asking them to join some sort of anti-partition movement. These letters in themselves are examples of the sort of ill-feeling and intolerance against which he was appealing. One such person, John C Crossle,[36] *wrote on 2 October 1935:*

Please do not assume that I have any dislike of Roman Catholics because of their religion. Far from it. I have very many friends amongst the Roman Catholic community for whom I have very warm regard. But we never discuss religion or politics as they and I know we should not agree and are content to remain good friends. I call anyone who refuses to acknowledge the King and Constitution a rebel and can never understand why they insist on living under a rule which they openly detest and insult on every occasion. It is indeed surprising to hear of Roman Catholics joining your Boy Scouts and saluting the flag. In all my experience they would not dream of doing so and the Union Jack dare not be seen in any Roman Catholic locality.

With the exception of a few ex-servicemen they refuse to acknowledge Armistice day, and would take no part in the

Jubilee celebrations. In Ballygawley their children were allowed to attend a fete on that day, but refused to take tea out of Jubilee mugs because they had pictures of the King and Queen on them. What would show more plainly their teaching: Irish Roman Catholics are entirely different to their co-religionists elsewhere and this can never be understood by people who have not lived amongst and mixed with them. I cannot see what more conciliation can be shown them than they have. They enjoy equal rights with the Protestant people and if they behaved as loyal citizens would be spared the rows they get into which are almost invariably started by themselves and when they reap the fruits they sow it is all Protestant intolerance and bigotry and make a terrible fuss. No, I did not read the *Ulster Protestant* but I know many people think it a great mistake to have such numbers of Roman Catholics in the RUC and Post Office. They have so often shown they are not to be trusted. All the troubles in this country are charged against Protestant people, never against the other side. I often wonder why.

But some of the letters gave a glimpse of better attitudes and a Church of Ireland Dean, Hugh MacManaway,[37] on 17 August 1935 wrote:

. . . We are heart and soul with you in the object you have in view. There are many people here who feel exactly as you and I do and who are willing to do anything in their power to create a spirit of friendship between all classes. Indeed, it is owing to the way we try to live together here as friends and neighbours that such peace and harmony exists. Thank God. There's a delightful atmosphere here. I attribute much of this feeling to the fact that the Roman Catholic Archdeacon and I are very good friends and can be seen now and again talking together in the street. People notice this sort of thing and it helps much. Next Tuesday afternoon I hope to go to Fr McQuade, Parish priest of Brookeboro, for tea. He was curate of Clogher when I was in Errigle, Keerogue and Ballygawley. If we could only have more of this sort of thing much good would follow in its train. . . . Personally I dislike politicians and nothing would induce me to go on an Orange platform to make a speech. Sir Basil and I promised each other to give up all that sort of thing some 20 years ago and I am sorry he was not able to keep his vow. However, I am convinced that there is much moderate opinion in Ulster and it should assert itself more vigorously in some way or other . . .

A Church of Ireland clergyman, Charles Cullimore,[38] *wrote:*

As one who always sympathised in my young Dublin days with Gladstone I would be delighted if you would consider the possibility I mentioned at your meeting of standing as a Dominion Unionist independently at the next vacancy. It might be a beginning of better days for our divided country. I am convinced that the true heart of Ireland – South as well as North – is not for separation of the Province, nor divorced from the great Commonwealth of free peoples which Irish men have done so much to create and preserve in the past. . . . Perhaps you could do something like this, for a still more important matter – the unity of the whole country within the British Commonwealth. Such a movement if at all successful would of itself soften religious asperities.

The remarkable thing which comes out of a study of this correspondence is the widespread goodwill and moderation expressed by people who would generally be held from their public utterances to be extremists. On 12 October Sir Robert Lynn,[39] *a Unionist MP, wrote:*

Many thanks for your kind letter. As a Protestant and Orangeman I feel I would be untrue to my principles if I did not preach toleration. Hatred of opponents is no part of the creed of a Protestant and it is unchristian.

In my native county – Antrim – we have never had physical quarrels with our Roman Catholic neighbours. Frankly, I cannot understand the outbreaks in Belfast and all men of goodwill should unite with the object of making them impossible. Loyalty will not thrive in an atmosphere of hatred. I have urged, even in the midst of the Sinn Fein murder campaign, that we must be scrupulously fair to the minority.

Our business is to do what is right regardless of what others may do or say. With kindest regards.

The doubts of well-intentioned people are well expressed in a letter of 30 August from another country gentleman, Hugh Montgomery Irwin,[40] *who was thoroughly pessimistic about the situation and in his analysis of the situation raised many of the points which those who thought in his vein raised in their letters also:*

I have so often thought out matters along the lines you suggest in your letter – but, alas, only in the end to dismiss them as hopelessly impracticable. The two main reasons which weighed with me were, firstly, the total want of any sympathisers with such ideas – in the circle, I know, only Verschoyle[41] and Burkitt[42] could be counted on at all and I should most probably soon differ from them in detail, secondly, the open and profound expression of disloyalty shown by so many Roman Catholics on every occasion which we hold dear, such as Armistice Day or the late Royal Wedding, and the attitude towards flying the Union Jack, tragic (if it was not so childish). As for Protestants among the small farmer class, such as my former tenants, I know of none, literally none, who have ever shown by word or deed anything approaching the ideas you seek to spread. And how could you expect them to be otherwise, when so many clergy openly belong to the Orange Order and profess, in many cases, the most extreme doctrines.

Assume for a moment we started the movement and organised some kind of an association, would not our fate be something like the Protestant Home Rulers in the last generation?[43] Remember the powers that be would stick at nothing if we in any way were successful, we should be branded (and all belonging to us) as disloyal traitors, and treated as social outcasts. But one might endure all this, if one was convinced that one *was* really conciliating some of the other side and saving them from being driven into extreme arms, but I am absolutely convinced from my work in the West ('19–'22)[44] and 12 years residence here that *one* thing the inhabitant of this unhappy country totally lacks is moral courage – they have none. They – that is to say – the Roman Catholics – are absolutely led by their priests (except the IRA!) quite a large number at my last election whispered to me 'I would vote for you but – well you know Father so and so says I must vote for Cahir Healy'[45] – What could any association we could form do towards these men? We should only earn the bitter hatred and boycott of our own people and the contempt of the leaders of the Nationalists. The only people who would (or might) welcome us would be the IRA, as in some way furthering their aim. In my very humble way I always have some Roman Catholics working on the place, and I hope I shall always be able to do so and I have refused and will always refuse to join the Orange Order, notwithstanding considerable pressure.

I feel very cowardly writing as I have done but it is my honest opinion – In my life in many parts of the world, I have never come across such peculiar conditions, as I met with on coming to live here. Never did I dream that I should see and encounter medieval history conditions repeated in modern times. Wipe out the Orange Order, abolish the priests' influence, and calm, cold reason might pervade, but at present you would preach to the Sahara Desert. You must be white or black, you cannot be gray! At our local Board of Guardians I sit at the other end of the long table opposite the chairman declining to sit on the left with the goats, or on the right with the sheep, a cold and lonely position, but as I usually disagree with both, not inappropriate!

As for the immediate cause – the late riots in Belfast – I am quite convinced it was deliberately planned by the IRA (and only stopped from being a much larger business by the action of the Civic Guards at Dundalk) to provoke the Orangemen and I do not blame them breaking out when six of their number were killed in cold blood before any of the others were hurt. We must be thankful the riots stopped when they did. Further, have the Roman Catholic authorities in any way condemned the firing on the Orange Procession? Have they shown one word of sympathy with these victims? Did they join our Bishop and the Moderator in preaching tolerance? Did one of their clergy openly follow the example of Dean Kerr? No, they waited until the worst was over and they had enough victims to make a harrowing appeal to English opinion and co-religionists in the South. It reminded me vividly of the Sinn Fein propaganda in '19–'22 – a campaign of exaggerations and half lies.

I am as down as you are on the action of so many leading men among us damning every Roman Catholic and excluding every one of them from every post of influence. I go further perhaps than you would in asserting that the only hope in the future is a United Ireland, even if only on a Federal basis, where the cold, hardheaded North will counterbalance the wild impulsiveness of the South. Ours is too artificial a state to last. No country ever lasted and became permanent with a perpetual dominant majority and no hope of a change of Government or an enjoyment of power. The minority have a perpetual grievance, as the two thirds have permanently distorted every constituency, every plan of voting from Senate to Board of Guardians to deprive the one third of their legitimate one third of power. No office from Coronership to Justice of the High Court is allowed to the one third – without a struggle – and, further, what makes it worse in my eyes is that those who should from birth and education be opposed are in most cases the leaders in furthering such action.

You say the Roman Catholics will be driven into permanent disloyalty. Why, they have been year by year since 1922. And I venture to say there are very few still to be driven. They are permanently disloyal and will remain so notwithstanding all our efforts, as long as they are treated as they are.

If, as originally intended, Donegal had been taken in, and there had been only a 10–15% majority instead of the present 2–1, there might have been some stability and hope, but if you read Carson's and Redmond's Lives you see how careful 'they' were to make things 'safe'.

Well, you must be sick of the sight of my handwriting and weary of my negative attitude but, though I am with you absolutely in your feelings, I am doubtful of your remedies.

A month later, after having discussed the matter with his friends, the same writer was even more pessimistic. He wrote on 24 September:

I am afraid they are all pessimists, agreeing up to the hilt with everything in theory, but fighting shy immediately any public action is proposed – what cowards we all are! On the other hand, personally I have added my voice two or three times in life to an unpopular cause, and every time been left high and

dry with much abuse and no thanks or success. Perhaps that
is why I am so 'cautious', or is it my Scotch ancestry, waiting
to see which way the cat is jumping?

But seriously, I see no basis whatsoever, no unleavened,
amorphous mass of people waiting to be kneaded and
moulded into some definite driving force of public opinion.

. . . It is very rare we have any religious rows here except in
a drunken brawl, though we are mixed 50/50 all over the
county. If this is so, where am I to start to preach? What reason am I to give for doing so? The 'gerrymandering' of the
local bodies, or party divisions – I should be laughed at and
asked what the milk board are doing with the money they take
away from the poor 'C' grade vendor. *That* question lies far
nearer to their heart than any abstract question of how he
should treat his neighbour.

The few farmers I have heard talk about the Belfast troubles all discuss them as if it were a remote foreign country and
wind up with 'oh, but they are always having rows up there'.
It does not directly affect them so why worry – from long standing we are far more in touch with, say, Sligo than, say, Belfast
or Derry – we know all about Monaghan and Cavan but Portadown and Lurgan leave us cold. We are *not* Northerners by
race or understanding. We may be Orangemen but of a *very*
mild type. . . . Dragoon both sides by an outside authority or
dictator – Yes. Transport *en bloc* one group or other (such as
Turkey and Greece did) – Yes. Seek to create a moderate common sense middle party – No – Never as long as human nature
is as it is and the clergy on both sides fan the flames. Sorry but
these are my opinions. . . .

*This feeling of helpless dismay was echoed by another Church of Ire-
land clergyman, William Kerr,[46] who wrote on 8 April 1935:*

I was brought up in the Free State and know how Roman
Catholics and Protestants can live in neighbourly friendship.
I find so different an atmosphere here *on both sides* that I am
at a loss to explain it but I think the main reason is political
fear and in a less sense the traditional religious fear. We must
remember that the Free State Protestants accept the Constitution. The Roman Catholics here are ever striving to upset it

and bring in an order that terrifies our people. Where I fear you are too optimistic is in thinking that any tolerance (right in itself) can ever make Roman Catholics loyal. I cannot envisage them, no matter how prosperous and well treated, as ever being aught but hostile to our Government and the Empire. (No matter how many Roman Catholic farmers suffer in the Free State they have only to be told they are fighting England and they go on voting insanely for DeValera.) Until they cease here to try to abolish what our people regard as their guarantee of freedom and liveable conditions then I fear bitterness will survive. Let the Roman Catholics accept the Constitution and you will see a blessed change.

Another thing not generally recognised is that in Belfast they bring their troubles on themselves. I do not defend the dangerous hooligan element we have, but I know that again and again the Roman Catholic aggressiveness, outrage and provocation are simply amazing. I often am astonished at their folly. As an outsider you could not realise it. The attacks and insults even in the main streets to all who displayed imperial emblems at the Jubilee were almost incredible.

All men of goodwill must strive for reconciliation. Until the majority can feel that they are not grappling in a life and death struggle with the opponents of their government, empire, religion and future of their children then progress will be slow.

A moderate Unionist view was expressed by businessman D E McCorkell[47] *from Londonderry in two letters. On 10 September he wrote:*

Please accept my apologies for having addressed my last letter wrongly. I have been thinking over the problem of tolerance – or the lack of it.

I am a strong supporter of our Government and could not take any part in any movement which would either tend to incline the Government further towards the extremist section or would help that section to pull down the existing political structure to replace it by a collection of ranting demagogues.

I do not think any of our leaders are bigots but unfortunately many of the small fry are and the franchise plays into their hands. While I have always been concerned with the question of where votes are cast and not where prayers are said, yet I cannot ignore the fact that the attitude of both the Nationalist Party and the Roman Catholic Church in Northern Ireland renders any *modus vivendi* difficult of attainment. The party from the inception of our Parliament has been not only obstructive but disruptive. The Church places barriers in the way of any negotiations, eg (i) lack of reciprocity, as in the case of mixed marriages, (ii) the assumption that they and they only are invariably right and, (iii) the dreadful weapon of mental reservation, which handicaps one at the beginning and leaves one in the dark at the end of any discussion.

If the Vatican owes anything to any Protestant state it is to England and judging by the Pope's message to the King at the Jubilee this is admitted, yet Rome has never supported the imperial idea in Ireland or, if it has, the hierarchy has completely broken loose. While I have always been in favour of Roman Catholics being helped to be good citizens, reflections of the above kind render the finding of a method very difficult. If some of their people would come forward and prove themselves constructive I feel sure our Government would welcome it. As things are I see little hope of anything being achieved except by decent examples of moderation being displayed by individuals on both sides. Any organised educational effort would probably be regarded as 'sedition' by some and as 'heresy' by others. I fear I am not very helpful but the problem is one which is so involved that efforts to solve it seem to be fraught with the danger of rendering it more 'active' than before.

I shall be very interested to hear of any progress which may be made and I trust we may see no more of disgraceful behaviour such as that in Belfast during the recent riots.

On 30 December he wrote again as follows:

Again I must apologise for delay in answering your letter. Both McFarland[48] and I have been away from home at various times and I have only recently had an opportunity of discussing with him your suggestion regarding a committee. He agrees with me that so far as he and I are concerned membership of such a committee would serve no useful purpose at this juncture.

It would probably merely result in our ostracism from our own party to which we are strongly attached. We both, as you know, have opinions as to the reasonable attitude which should be adopted with regard to our opponents. In 'the wilderness' we could do nothing. As it is we feel that a decent example of 'clean fighting' can accomplish more for the well-being of the community than an organisation which would probably be misconstrued as regards its motives, with consequent bad results.

I find that there is a considerable number of people who are anxious that affairs should be conducted on sane and constitutional lines; the great majority of these agree with me that a reasonable attitude displayed by individuals is likely to be more successful than any effort to form new parties or to embarrass our own in which there are a great many people *in all sections* who deplore fanaticism and 'dirty work'.

I fear the Nationalists of Tyrone and Fermanagh have done little to pour oil on the troubled waters,[49] as their recent action suggests that they are, to all intents and purposes, of much the same kidney as the Republicans whom they attack at times, when it suits them. I may be wrong but it strikes me they threw away a great opportunity if they have indeed any constitutional vision. Instead of returning two 'Abstentionists' they might themselves have abstained from voting and then given the lie to those who say 'They are all the same; not a whit of difference between any of them'.

When we meet I think, however, that I could tell you some things (perhaps already known to you) which give promise of an effort to prevent extremists from acting in a manner disgraceful to themselves and prejudicial to the Unionist cause which we both have at heart.

Montgomery received a more conservative response from the Secretary of the Ulster Unionist Council, Sir Wilson Hungerford,[50] in a letter of December 1935:

I am afraid I cannot share the view that 'constitutional' Nationalists, if treated in a different way would not unite themselves with Republicans and others who are trying to 'down' the Northern Government. No doubt their tactics may not be so violent but their object is the same.

The letters quoted above represent most of the points of view put for-
ward in the correspondence which Montgomery received in response
to his appeal in August. The interpretation of his attitude varied from
those who saw in it Irish Nationalism, to those who accepted him as
a staunch Unionist who did not appreciate the impractical nature of
his aims. Among the replies received by Montgomery was a long letter
(September 7, 1935) from a retired British diplomat, Sir Robert
Kennedy,[51] *which applauded Montgomery's aims, criticised the Stor-*
mont Government and suggested a plan of action which Montgomery
might follow:

My dear General. I take advantage of a quiet day previous to
my departure for three or four weeks. Now that all my family,
wife, children and grandchildren, together with servants and
outdoor labourers have all hurried off to the TT motor races,
in which I take no interest, to write to you on the subject of
your most interesting letter and proposed propaganda. It
must, as you seem wisely to realise, be dealt with like the bap-
tism of an infant 'warily and discreetly', or like marriage not
be lightly 'undertaken', but, all the same, it ought not to be
shirked.

First of all as regards the Prime Minister I saw him yesterday at the aviation meeting at Newtownards. He was most amiable to me personally, but my conversation with him, as it
generally is, was platitudinous. He always seems to be on his
guard with me and avoids coming to close quarters on any discussion of the many problems with which we are all con-
fronted. He told me that motor driving accidents are
increasing but when I remarked that this is largely due to
Northern Ireland want of manners arising from defective educational training, especially in our schools, he shied off!

But between you and me we must, for the present, put up
with him, on the principle followed many years ago in France
when a new President was elected and was nicknamed 'Mon-
sieur le Président Faute de Mieux'.

I do not know Basil Brooke personally, but Herbert Dixon
(I say it with regret, as by marriage he is closely connected with
me) is a notorious 'twister'. I make out D Bates[52] as an uneducated Belfast cad, at the mercy of the Stormont bureaucracy

and of Sir C Wickham.[53] The latter owes his position to the fact that his first wife was a close friend of Lady Craigavon, but I believe (you would know best) that as a military officer in a munitions regiment he was quite undistinguished. Moreover as an Englishman he does not understand Northern Ireland characteristics – he in his heart despises Orangemen and is disliked by them. This makes his position uncomfortable to say the least.

Milne Barbour[54] is amiable and honourable – John Andrews is conscientious and hard working – but neither carry much weight. Pollock[55] is a good financial accountant for all local purposes but he is old, more cranky and tactless. They and all the clique of under secretaries etc are saturated with the spirit of 'team work' ie slavish subservience to the Prime Minister and to Dawson Bates.

Our Parliament is composed of men who are either in receipt of handsome salaries or who are on the look-out for 'loaves and fishes' for themselves and their friends, so they are cautious in criticism, and the 'opposition' is hopelessly heterogeneous and therefore quite useless. In plain words our Parliament instead of being a safeguard is a positive danger to public democratic liberty.

I will go a step further and tell you in *sacred confidence* that I suspect that our Prime Minister whose eminent services in former years I most fully recognise, is, with increasing years, suffering from a hardening of the arteries, commonly called 'arthritis', an incurable malady which kills everyone except the patient! I have seen it in three cases in private life with which I have been connected. In that malady the sufferer becomes unreasonably obstinate, perverse, and incapable of seeing anything except from his own point of view – in one word – impossible! Therefore I agree with you when you say 'I am inclined to think that he shall do no good till he goes but who is to take his place?'

Ah! That is the rub! Because, with infinite cunning the Prime Minister has crossed off suitable men of mature age from public life and discouraged young men from coming forward as under-studies. Our local press, too, is a source of weakness, and we also have to bear in mind that we are in the

position of a local garrison holding the fort against our enemies not only at our gates but also sapping and mining under
our defences. That fort is 'loyalty to the King, and the
supremacy of the State over the Church – any Church – in a
spirit of Christian toleration'. The danger is the Irish Republican, and (as Gambetta once said when he hunted monks and
nuns out of France across the English Channel) 'Le Clérical-
isme voilà l'Ennemi'.

Now for some practical though I fear crude suggestions. You
say that in your opinion our course should be 'some quiet propaganda with occasional letters to the press when good open-
ings occur' followed by a manifesto 'signed by a few influential
backers'.

Presumably I should advise not writing your local press –
letters provoke rude and vulgar criticism – anonymous, of
course, which cause bad blood – they are controversial by uneducated men who have little knowledge and no manners.

What we want is not controversy but education in simple
language, at first: 'milk' before 'strong meat' and it might take
the forms of careful thoughtful leaflets on various subjects,
such as:

'Religious Toleration. What does it mean?'
'Civic Duties. What are they?'
'The Orange Order. Its origin and principles.'
'Liberty not Licence. Live and let live.'
'The Duties and Responsibilities of Parliament.'

At first these leaflets should be unsigned, and should not
be sent to the local press, but scattered like seed in various
more or less sympathetic quarters. Later on, if the ground thus
prepared seems suitable there might be a more ambitious
manifesto or declaration more or less on the lines of some of
the able articles in newspapers of the *Spectator* class. We have
no monthly or weekly cheap paper animated by a desire to
raise the tone of public thought and to create a healthy public opinion. A newspaper like *The Belfast Telegraph* which has
an enormous circulation deliberately, in order to make money,
panders to the passions of the multitude.

Our hope lies with the younger generation educated in pub-

lic schools of the Campbell College type. I am one of the gov-
ernors and I have been greatly struck by the great improve-
ment in style, manners, tone and knowledge of the young men
turned out of the College to take their place in universities,
army and learned professions as well as in commercial life.

Our trouble in Northern Ireland is the aloofness of the
Church of Rome. The hierarchy and the priests refuse to take
any part in our public life, I mean in secular matters. I have
never seen any of them at any social function – they will not
even attend a public dinner or luncheon at the City Hall given
by the Lord Mayor in honour of Royalty or distinguished
British statesmen. Their whole system of education tends to
emasculate virility and from childhood a Roman Catholic boy
is taught to hate and boycott a Protestant boy. But when in
later life a mixed marriage takes place stern orders, in defiance
of the laws of the State, are given that all children of the marriage shall be brought up as Roman Catholics.

In England the Roman Catholic Church acts more cau-
tiously and warily, so our trouble is not realised by our English friends. In some of our dominions, New Zealand, for
instance, it is a penal offence for the Church of Rome to take
up a hostile attitude of this kind against the State.

This is one of the main points that might be skilfully and
delicately dealt with in such a leaflet as I have suggested, and
it would have effect, because as a prominent English peer once
said to me when during the Carson anti-Home Rule agitation,
before the war, I addressed crowded meetings in the Albert
Hall, Caxton Hall, etc in London 'If you can rouse the Protestant feeling in England you will kill Home Rule'.

The Roman Catholic republics of South America have not
formally but in practice broken away from the thraldom of the
Church of Rome. When I was British Minister Plenipotentiary
at Montevideo the Minister for Foreign Affairs, a Roman
Catholic of Spanish origin, asked me if his son could be admitted into our British School at Montevideo. I readily agreed,
adding that the boy would be excused from attending morning prayers or any divinity classes upon which he replied:
'Nothing that a boy hears or learns in a British school can do
him any harm'!

Will the day ever dawn when such a spirit of broad Christian toleration, either Protestant or Roman Catholic, will be established in this narrow-minded country of Ireland? That is the goal for which slowly we must work.

Pray excuse the length of this letter. If you have the patience to wade through it, and if you think that our Bishop of Down in whose tact, wisdom, and above all, discretion, I have the fullest confidence, would care to see it, I have no objection to you showing it to him in confidence.

On 19 September the News Letter *published a letter from Montgomery in which he stated clearly the aims which he had in mind, shows why he believed the minority have a grievance and why he thought it was in the interest of the majority to do something to create a better atmosphere and better relations. The letter was as follows:*

During the past fortnight two noble contributions have been made to the cause of peace and goodwill by members of the Northern Government:

(i) The Prime Minister's emphatic condemnation at Bessbrook of any attempt to victimise Roman Catholics on account of their religion; in this he will have the whole Unionist party solidly behind him.

(ii) The Minister of Labour's reminder at Comber that 'Civil and religious liberty for all' applies to 'our opponents as well as ourselves, provided they act constitutionally and keep within the laws of the land'.

The loyal acceptance of these two presentments should go a long way to establish the better relations which every good Protestant would like to see.

But this acceptance involves a principle on which they have not in the past been in general agreement, namely a clear recognition of the fact that 'our opponents', that is, those who vote against us, are acting in a perfectly constitutional manner in so doing.

One might, I think, go further and say that one could hardly expect anything else; their homes have for our convenience been included in the area of Northern Ireland without their having been consulted, and in many cases against their will, and it is quite natural that they should have taken such steps as were legally open to them to protest.

They know, however, that Protestants here cannot consent to go under a Dublin Parliament and that sooner or later they will have to accept the situation and make the best of it.

Whether they accept it sooner or later will depend chiefly on the kind of treatment they receive from us and therefore quite apart from the question of Christian goodwill between neighbours it is clearly to the advantage of our Province, which can never be really flourishing until we have all learned to pull together, that they should be treated with courtesy and consideration – so long as they keep within the bounds of the law.

This letter sums up very clearly the position which Montgomery wished to maintain. It was a position open to misinterpretation from both sides but its essential sense and moderation made a strong appeal to moderate people. By November 1935 Charlemont and Montgomery were discussing the form which the proposed organisation might take and Charlemont expressed his views with a brevity, wit and shrewdness which were typical of him. On 13 November he wrote:

Yes, I saw your letter as published and needless to say agreed with it. I am not sure that the best course of action for the ABC would not be to ascertain the people who are in sympathy with the general aims of the movement and meet occasionally to talk things over. The formation of 'cells', that is. The Bolsheviks of Russia started things on that line and it was successful enough.

All this time Montgomery was a member of the Unionist party and of the Ulster Unionist Council. In January 1936 he made a speech there in which he put his point of view very forcefully and very succinctly.

In his remarks at the Standing Committee, Montgomery commented on certain paragraphs in the report which said that the distinction which had formerly been drawn between Constitutional Nationalists and extremists or Republicans could no longer be made. This struck at the very core of Montgomery's views for he insisted (as in his letter to the News *Letter) that constitutional opposition within the law was perfectly correct behaviour. He said:*

It seems to me that the theory evolved in these two paragraphs [of the report] based on the General Election that practically all the Nationalists have thrown in their lot with the Republicans, and that there is no difference between the two, does not hold good except perhaps in portions of Belfast. Take Tyrone and Fermanagh, for instance: here we had the Nationalists deliberately deciding that they would not be represented in Parliament *at all*, rather than be represented by Republicans.

Even if this theory was a good deal more plausible than it is, I think it is a most shortsighted mistake to let it go out in an official document of this kind that, in future, Roman Catholics (or Nationalists, if you like) are to be considered as being on exactly the same footing whether they are rebellious or law-abiding.

I go further; I think it is suicidal, because in the long run our survival as a separate entity will depend on our being able to establish some kind of *modus vivendi* with these people.

The Prime Minister has laid it down that, for his time, the Government of Ireland Act has closed a chapter in the history of this country which will not be re-opened. If that is so, it means that, for many years to come, we shall have some 400,000 Roman Catholics living in our midst. What attitude are we going to adopt towards them? We can't extirpate them, as was attempted in the time of Queen Elizabeth. We can't evict them, as was done in the reign of James I. We can't drive them across the border into Connaught, like Cromwell did. And, we can't disfranchise them, as was done all through the 18th century.

As we have got to live alongside these people, I think we might try whether a little more *goodwill* might not produce some effect; and a policy of conciliation towards those who are prepared to be reasonable, combined with the suppression of those who are not.

This, I am confident, would be the policy adopted towards a minority like this in every other part of the Empire. It is also the policy indicated in the excellent paragraph which begins at the foot of page seven and goes on to page eight: 'The Ulster Government . . . extends toleration to all religious beliefs sin-

cerely held, and political opinions constitutionally expressed'
and 'The distinction between liberty and licence is clean-cut.'

Now the two paragraphs I have referred to on page five are
quite inconsistent with this policy; and their tendency is rather
to blur than to accentuate the 'clean-cut'.

I would therefore recommend that they should be omitted.

*In a letter of 18 January Charlemont commented on Montgomery's
argument:*

I am not sure, however, that I agree with you on the Nationalists–Republican matter. While I am certain that a very large
number of Nationalists do not like absenteeism, how many of
them abstained from voting Republican. Very few indeed, I
would say, and a man must be known by his votes as far as
politics are concerned. The principle of toleration, however,
would not be affected by that, so long as the Republican keeps
the law of the land in which he lives he should not suffer for
his opinions.

*He went on to quote Cromwell who said 'the State in choosing men
to serve takes no notice of their opinions if they are willing to serve it
faithfully, that satisfies'.*

*During 1936 the cell idea which Charlemont propounded at the
end of 1935 seems to have been put into effect. Apparently in January 1936 Montgomery had addressed a group of people gathered
together by an Enniskillen clergyman who was organising a group of
six people in the hope that it would increase in size later on. He asked
Montgomery to 'please tell me what I shall do next with the committee
and I promise you I shall answer your letter'. He referred to the fact
that Montgomery had such a good meeting in Omagh – apparently
little meetings had been held throughout the west at least. In June he
had been speaking in a country house in County Londonderry where
a group of people had been gathered; for his hostess was writing saying how much they had all enjoyed the meeting and suggested that one
might be held in a country house in County Armagh next month. She
wrote: 'A series of such gatherings will affect public opinion, of course
there is some criticism; some say that the past should not be recalled
but surely it must be salutatory to be aware of the true facts of our past
injustices and rapacity though it may not be pleasant. That is very
different from raising up past differences inflicted on us by others....'*

Henry Dobbs, a friend in County Antrim, was finding the going rather hard and in February 1936 complained that he had found people less responsive than he had hoped.

I know you will be wondering why I have not written again to you on the 'toleration' subject and I must apologise for not having done so.

The truth is that I waited, first of all, to get an opportunity of talking the matter over with Hugh O'Neill[56] as I pinned a good deal of faith on the value of his support. I did see him about a fortnight ago, and was frankly disappointed at his attitude. To begin with, I found out that he had already heard from you on the subject, which was unfortunate, as I had hoped to find 'Virgin soil' instead of which I gathered the impression that he had already come to definite conclusions.

I am sorry you didn't let me know you had written to him. If you have done so to any others in these parts please let me know who they are, as it makes a difference to one's line of attack.

To revert to O'Neill, I think it is a fair summing up of his position to say that he feels that we are inclined to saddle the Orangemen and Unionists with too much of the responsibility for the present situation, whereas he considers that the Roman Catholics are far more responsible. Secondly, he is definitely of the opinion that the state of affairs in Belfast is much more due to 'gangster' tendencies than to the politics–religious feelings of the general run of citizens.

Now I have quoted O'Neill (as I remember his words) at some length because he is in my view typical of the best Protestant opinion in these parts, and would undoubtedly carry much weight. If this is so, it will be a great deal more difficult than I thought to get much support. I will, however, certainly try before giving up hope of some small success.

O'Neill also told me that the position in Belfast was more acute than ever and that the fanatics on both sides were doing their best to make things difficult for the Government. This again is not a favourable symptom.

On 5 February Lord Charlemont wrote once more to point out some of the problems which he believed the ABC would face:

Wherever you get a considerable number of Catholics in a population there you will have the meddling priest, the everlasting *urge* to get the Protestant well under, to extinction, if possible. I think it's a real danger, and I really have ideas about the Roman *Church* that are quite worthy of an Orangeman!

What, therefore, is the future of the ABC? I don't know. If the ABC were to remove tomorrow all feelings of Protestant versus Catholic, the Catholic Church would press for *superiority* and make it a grievance if they were denied it. You can see this with great clarity in education, which I needn't go into.

The individual Roman Catholic will sometimes co-operate, but his church never – and is *opposed* to co-operation. Your mixed school,[57] for instance, hangs on a thread. I have, apparently, been able to bluff your priest, but if your Roman Catholic bishop is inclined the way I think he is, he will be at your priest again and I don't know if the latter is made of very stern stuff.

And look at Stranmillis Training College! Some few years ago I almost got the Roman Catholic bishops to allow their men entrants to the teaching profession to enter it, the Roman Catholic Bishop of Down being a little more progressive and sensible than his fellows. They were to have a hostel of their own and clergy of their own attached to it, and Heaven knows what else to remove them from Protestant contamination – and then they said they must have *playing fields* of their own! I am afraid I think that the Roman Catholic Church in Ireland will always be against us *whatever* we do, and if the ABC was really on the point of effecting a conciliation they would put a spanner in the works – and keep a supply of spanners!

It's possible that the Roman Catholic Church has been brought to this state by Penal Laws which applied in England as well, but we have to take things as they *are*. I think the best plank the ABC have in their platform is the effect of intransigent speeches on English opinion. No one can argue against this point of view; it's a fact, and Billy Grant may think it's deplorable of the English and it may be, but it is a fact for all that – and might be a determining factor in their support of us. I am rather pessimistic about the Ulster future. Not being in politics, you may think that Basil [Brooke] and Billy and Sir

Joseph Davison and all that lot are impelled to make their speeches from Protestant fervour, and one might ask why they have only started to make them in the last years or so. It's not entirely religious fervour – it's the gradual increase of pressure from independent organisations, leagues, Socialism; all the political expressions of Ulster individualism.

For the first ten years of self-government the hurrah boys and their friends kept Unionist MPs in their seats. But we're used to self-government now. . . . This is the trend of present politics, and unless the Herodianism of the Protestant League can be out-Heroded, I, a supporter of the Government, will lose my seat to a jackanapes, and with it, my chances of preferment. . . .

Why is Charlemont a moderate? Temperament is no doubt involved, but it mustn't be forgotten that he is a Senator and has no seat to maintain! With a few exceptions I think human beings are wonderfully *good* considering what temptations they are up against but their goodness is kept for their families and their friends and those others they are brought into daily contact with; on public platforms they are apt to be amazingly selfish and opportunist.

I do not think, anyhow, that the ABC will be able to compete much with the forces I have mentioned above, at any rate, not on their own ground. It can get together a small nucleus of sensible opinion and hope that it may become the little leaven that will leaven the whole mass.

Montgomery did not confine his activity to drawing-room meetings. He was an indefatigable letter-writer and wrote on every possible occasion to the press and to individuals who had spoken in public and expressed views with which he disagreed. Following is the reply (15 September 1936) of a Londonderry clergyman, J Godfrey MacManaway,[58] *to a letter in which Montgomery had obviously criticised his sermon:*

It was a pleasure to get a letter from you this morning, even though in criticism. I do not mind criticism in the slightest, provided that it is fair and I know that you would always strive to be that.

I think you must have read that extract from my sermon which appeared in the *News Letter* very hurriedly, however.

(i) The tone of my sermon was in no way affected by the presence of the Prime Minister. I preached a much stronger sermon a few weeks before when he was not there, it was fully reported in the local press. I do not know if it appeared elsewhere.

(ii) You say that the tone of the sermon was 'un-Christian and bitter . . . not a word of goodwill towards opponents from beginning to end'. Now I turn to the *News Letter* report and I read these words 'We wish to live here in peace and amity with all men . . . we desire prosperity for all our citizens of whatever creed or class, we have no wish to interfere with the civil or religious liberties of anyone'. Now, General, even from the abridged report in the *News Letter* how could you make the statement that there was not one word of goodwill towards our opponents from beginning to end?

(iii) You also know something about controversy (I am being candid as you desired). It is always unsafe to make unqualified charges. For instance, you had not seen my sermon in full before you wrote those sweeping statements. Now, if you had you would have known that there was still less ground for what you assert than even now appears. Again towards the end of my sermon I said 'We have no ill-will whatever towards any man on the score of his religion. It is not our fault that most rebels belong to a different faith from our own – that is purely incidental. We respect, and always will respect, the religious convictions of our Roman Catholic neighbours' etc, etc. I ask you were the statements lacking in goodwill, were they un-Christian? If not, what becomes of your criticism?

(iv) You make a reference to somebody called 'old Bingham'. Who this worthy is I don't know. But to drag in a statement to buttress your case from a man who cannot be challenged either to substantiate or withdraw because your letter is marked 'Personal' is a most unfair procedure.

(v) Now, in actual fact, every word of criticism on my part in my sermon was directed against rebels, that was made abundantly clear. Do you object to rebels being criticised? I have never in my life attacked any form of religion, no matter what I may think about it, but I frequently attack and will continue to do so those who preach treason and disloyalty no matter what brand of faith they profess. If you lived here in Derry as I do you would know that instead of criticising me for what I said, you should give me credit for what I did not say. I have two churches here. One of them is close to but not in a Roman Catholic area. Every Sunday for many years we have to have police on duty outside owing to crowds gathering and throwing stones at the church. Some time ago, three children, parishioners of mine, were kidnapped here in broad daylight and placed in the Nazareth Home. Since then two more children have been kidnapped. Will you tell me, what would happen if we Protestants stoned Roman churches and kidnapped Roman children – either here or in the Free State? Can't you imagine how the world would ring with shrieks of 'Orange atrocities' and the action that would be taken? Thank goodness our people – the supposed bigots – do not retaliate in any way. I could make plenty of authentic revelations as to how we 'Protestants' are treated by our opponents in Derry City, but if I did nothing could prevent retaliation in other places.

As regards the Free State, General, and the way our people are treated there – I know as much as any man in Ireland. I happen to be Chairman for five years of an organisation which exists to give financial aid to distressed Protestants in the Free State.[59] I can, if necessary, produce the facts and figures showing what success our people have had there in obtaining work. I am there every week in this connection. On Friday I shall (D V) be in Cork on that business. I shall give you only one instance – I can give you scores if you wish. Last month the proprietor of a well known motor garage in Dublin needed a foreman. The proprietor is himself one of us. He took on a Protestant. He was immediately boycotted for three weeks and, at last, had to let the man go. Now, if you wish it, I shall give you all the details so that you may verify for yourself. This is not an isolated case – I have the files here full of them, and coming in every month. I would refer you also to the words of Dr Fogarty, Roman Catholic Bishop of Killaloo, six weeks ago: 'Unless you belong to a certain party there is no hope of obtaining employment here'. The party he referred to is DeValera's. I need not say that very few Protestants in the Irish Free State

belong to that party. Last week I was at Clonmel in Tipperary.
I met a party of Protestant clergy and laity. In response to my
questions I was told that Protestants have very little hope of
employment. I am as familiar with the statements of some
Protestant clergy in the Free State as anyone. I know what Mr
Boyd said, I know what two of our bishops said. But all the
statements in the world will not overthrow the facts. The next
time you see a similar statement from a Free State bishop or
clergyman, I suggest you write and put the following questions
to him:

(i)   Is your population dwindling?

(ii)   If so, is it partly due to your young people leaving the
       Free State to seek employment elsewhere?

(iii) If so, why are they doing so?

The fact is, General, as regards these things bishops are not
the best sources of information for the simple reason that it
is not part of their duty to try and put Protestants into employment and hence they are unaware of the difficulties. They
speak quite sincerely but, if the truth be told, sometimes without accurate knowledge of the facts.

There are others, whom we need not waste time upon, who
speak up in the North with a view to the effect of their words
in the South. I would not say this, if I were not travelling over
the Free State every month on this very mission and with facts
and figures from every county. Last week I myself interviewed
the secretary of a large organisation in Dublin with a view to
getting some ex-servicemen into employment. I know the secretary well. He is a Roman Catholic. He told me quite candidly 'Neither Protestants nor ex-servicemen are wanted in
the Free State'. Now having told you a little of what I know
and can substantiate you will perhaps understand that I am in
as good a position as most men to know accurately just how
our people fare down South.

As regards 'gerrymandering' wards here in Derry City – we
certainly are and, in my opinion, with every justification. When
an alien population is deliberately poured into our area from
the Free State with the one object of getting control of the
City, we can only take such constitutional means as are avail-

able to prevent the success of this hostile plan. Several thou-
sand Roman Catholics have come into Derry from the Irish
Free State in the last ten years and still they come. Unless we
get power to ban their entry altogether we must take steps to
see that they do not succeed in their one object – undermin-
ing our position as an integral part of Northern Ireland. While
on the subject of 'gerrymandering' – I suggest that you read
the article on the Free State in that very sober quarterly *The
Round Table* in the current issue.[60] If you do so, you will see
that so far as that political manoeuvre is concerned we are but
learners here as compared with the politicians on the other
side of the border. Not that I uphold 'gerrymandering' as a
principle, but it is forced upon us here by our opponents
employing tactics which were never foreseen or provided for
when our democratic institutions were set up. You will find in
the New Testament itself that deepest of all principles, namely
that human necessity knows no law. Now you refer to the
'beams' in our eye, which should be attended to.

I hope, if you write again, that you will say what these 'beams'
are. Personally, I am unaware of them. So far as we Protestants
are concerned, we treat the Roman Catholic minority in the
North with a tolerance that is not afforded to minorities in
any other country. For instance, it is a Government regulation
that of all those employed on Public Relief schemes one third
must be Roman Catholics.[61] Do you know of any similar provision for the minority in any country of the world? Last year
I visited New Zealand, Australia and South Africa. I enquired
in those countries as to the educational regulations with
regard to their Roman Catholic citizens. In not one of them
is the special provision made for them which we make here.
Again, I must ask, what are the 'beams' you refer to. If I said
anything in my sermon which was not absolutely true I hope
you will tell me what that was. But, if not, why reproach me? I
don't know who the 'Billy Boys' are that you refer to, but I
should probably prefer them to the Free State gunmen. As
regards Sir Basil Brooke, he used an indiscreet phrase, but in
my opinion what he said was true enough. He should have
said 'Disloyalists' not Roman Catholics, but, as you and I know,
unhappily the two descriptions happen to refer to the same

people where Ireland is concerned. Exceptions only serve to prove the general rule. Now, in conclusion, I would like to tell you this. I stood beside my best friend, Lieutenant Jack Wogan-Browne, an Irishman and a Roman Catholic, when he was foully murdered by Sinn Fein gunmen in the streets of Dublin. From that day to this I have waged 'war' on rebels. Their religion is a matter of indifference to me. I shall continue to speak the truth as I see it, without fear or favour. I am sure you will do the same. The important thing is – not that we should necessarily agree – but that we should respect each other's motives.

It was against such feeling, by propaganda among a limited group of people that Montgomery sold the idea of the Irish Association. Foundations were laid in 1935 and 1936 although Charlemont's correspondence continued to warn of possible dangers. On 23 October 1936 he wrote to Montgomery saying:

. . . It must be remembered that the Protestants have been through a Papist rebellion not so *very* long ago, and the outstanding feature of these times were that you couldn't *trust* a Papist. Two labourers of mine, for instance, who were actually on my property at the time burned down a house belonging to me! I, of course, with education and some understanding, reflected that had I been placed in the labourers' position between the upper millstone of general Protestant suspicion and the nether millstone of a militant IRA I might have equally been tempted to justify myself with the latter by destroying property for which I knew the owner would get compensation. But it would be foolish to expect that the average man in the street would have sufficient education or knowledge to have similar reflections. He would merely say – 'Don't employ Roman Catholics for their employment won't prevent them from doing the dirty should they think it advisable.' I don't see how this feeling can ever be cured as it rests on fact. But governments should avoid any *manifestation* of their feelings which they have as ordinary men, and the same applies to corporations. I will have to talk to Milne Barbour next week; and even Basil [probably McFarland] lacks enthusiasm for the scheme.

THE CALL FOR SACRIFICE

Angel "get down from the tree, boy, an pat that bull. You can't make friends with him up there, and if you don't he'll go and hurt that gentleman over there."

1937–9
Foundation of the Association

In 1937 Montgomery was apparently asked to address a group of students at Queen's University and as a result of this an article by him on 'Ulster and the Empire' appeared in the June issue of the University Magazine New Northman. *This initiated more directly the formation of the Irish Association as it eventually developed and as it was actually founded as a going concern in 1938. Charlemont eventually became President of the Irish Association but he constantly gave Montgomery advice which boiled down to exhorting him to keep his feet on the ground and to be practical. Charlemont always proclaimed that he was a staunch Unionist, as indeed he was and part of his attitude towards the Irish Association (or the ABC as it was called by him and Montgomery before 1938 when it was only a figment in their imagination) is summed up in a cartoon which he drew and a letter which he wrote about it in July 1937.*

In the cartoon Charlemont shows two fields. In one is a figure of a man marked 'John Bull' surrounded by tanks, aeroplanes and artillery. In the other field is a tree with a bull at its base marked 'Irish Free State' and perched on a branch of the tree where he has taken refuge a young man marked 'Ulster'. An angel marked 'ABC' is hovering over the bull and the young man and saying to the young man 'Get down from the tree, boy, and pat that bull. You can't make friends with him up there and if you don't he'll go and hurt that gentleman over there', that gentleman being, of course, John Bull surrounded by his tanks, aeroplanes and artillery.

In the letter accompanying this cartoon Charlemont wrote:

I think the ABC is going too far in suggesting that Ulster should come down from the tree and start making concessions to the bull. To abandon metaphor, we have got a little independent state and it's safe enough at present. But it's much smaller and less powerful than the Free State and it would be well if the latter started concession-making by being silent about partition for a good bit. I do not believe that the inclusion of Ulster in the Free State – even complete inclusion – would make the least difference in the latter's attitude to England in a war. The Irish would always have a grievance of some kind and a great number of them would show it by helping England's enemies in any way they could. So I'm not in favour of any material sacrifice on Ulster's part. I'd just like to see Ulster leaving the Free State alone, though the habit of lecturing other states is not confined to Ulster! I think the ABC would be likely to alienate many sympathisers by suggesting concessions to the Irish Free State on the part of any Ulster Government; what it should work for is a better feeling between North and South for in the long run the heart is stronger than the head. If we could really attain, in the course of years, 'Hearts across the border', concessions on both sides would follow.

I'm going to Bundoran today for a week or so, and will possibly return carrying a white, orange and green flag!*

The problem of Unionist relations with Catholics in Northern Ireland and the Republic which the Irish Association was to address in subsequent years was perhaps best presaged by a letter from Montgomery to Basil Brooke in December 1935. He wrote:

I am always ready to agree to differ; but I should like you to realise that it is on methods and not on aims that we do differ. It is just because I believe that the policy of encouraging a cleavage between our majority and our minority, and antagonising the more moderate members of the latter, *is* going to 'smash the Constitution' before many years are up, that I am opposed to it. The crux will probably come after the next General Election when it will be asked 'How has the Protestant majority in Ulster treated the Roman Catholic minority placed under its control?'

It will be little use then arguing that the Government's administration has been progressive and impartial if they can point to speeches by Cabinet ministers and other leading men advocating a wholesale boycott [of Catholics].

I have talked to a good many responsible people lately about

* The Lecture to the Association in 1962 by Kenneth Darwin ended here.

this and I was surprised how many, especially among the younger generation, agree with me. However, I won't press the point any further *quat homines!*

It could be argued that Montgomery's prediction was correct in all but the date.

Although Montgomery continued to participate in meetings of small groups of friends and like-minded individuals in the following months it was not until mid 1938 that his ideas for a formal body were first aired publicly. On 2 July, when Montgomery mentioned the idea after a lecture given by Professor Henry at Queen's University, Belfast, it was clear from his statements that his ideas on the nature and objectives of the association had crystallised. On 4 July the Irish News *reported:*

A proposal that an association, non-political and non-sectarian, should be formed to promote better feeling between Eire and Northern Ireland is under consideration, declared Major-General Hugh Montgomery, of County Tyrone, speaking on Saturday at the Irish University Students' Association Congress in Belfast.

'We should make some effort to remove the obsession of the past in Ireland today,' he said, 'and social unity would leave constitutional and political questions to solve themselves. We must combat misrepresentation and intolerance, and encourage greater social intercourse between the North and South.

Professor R M Henry, of Queen's University, Belfast, who gave an address on 'A community obsessed by the past can have no hope for the future,' said that the trouble with Ireland was that she had too many pasts and traditions. The most important result of excessive preoccupations with the past was the idea that there were certain things it was now impossible to change. . . .

In a subsequent debate Major-General Hugh Montgomery, CB, CMG, DL, of Fivemiletown, County Tyrone, outlined a plan for promoting better feeling between North and South. He felt, he said, that something more definite might come out of the meeting than a mere resolution. 'Ireland,' he continued, 'is obsessed by the past, and anyone who has read Irish history will not be surprised.' He and a few friends had considered the matter for some years past and thought of starting an association to promote co-operation between all sections.

The association would be non-party and non-sectarian and would unite all those who desired to promote better relations between Irishmen. He had the idea that if this was done the political and constitutional problems of Ireland would solve themselves.

They had in mind to publish a leaflet stating the aims of the association. The members would meet to discuss their differences in reasonableness. Respect for the opinions of others would be encouraged. A wider cultural interest in the history and literature of Ireland would be promoted. The association would arrange for more social intercourse between people from all over Ireland and remove obstacles to better understanding.

Unfortunately the Irish News *itself seemed to have missed Montgomery's point, that the proposed association would be about improving relations between North and South, not about Irish political unity. The newspaper's editorial entitled 'Irish Social Unity' began by welcoming Montgomery's proposal but quickly retreated into traditional nationalism:*

The establishment of an association on the lines suggested by General Hugh Montgomery at the Irish Students' Congress in Belfast on Saturday, to promote better feeling between Irishmen, North and South, would be welcomed by the majority of the people of the country. Its reception would be none the less cordial by reason of its determination to let political and constitutional questions solve themselves.

But it would be well to realise that the difficulties confronting such an association would be tremendous. At first sight it might seem to the outsider that a political barrier should not interfere with the non-political interests of men of the same race. But in fact every possible effort has been made on the Northern side to keep the people apart, so that the dividing line of the Border might be found in every activity in which they are engaged.

Thus it is that Partition has created splits and disunion in sport, in education, and in many trade and professional organisations. In the few cases where an understanding exists between North and South it is grim necessity that has demanded co-operation. The police forces of 'Ulster' and Eire may join in the hunt for a criminal. But the social amenities lay a trap for the unwary Ulsterman who may find himself in company where the Royal toast is not drunk and the Union Jack does not appear.

If the new organisation suggested by General Montgomery is strong enough to defy cheap sneers and ignorant criticism it will make good progress. To ensure success, it should be mindful of Professor Henry's words, also spoken at the Irish Students' Congress, about Ireland and her past, and break away from the inglorious past of 'Ulster' that has been responsible for so much mischief and disruption in the hope of keeping the border fixed forever.

The Unionist reaction to Montgomery's kite-flying, rather than being hostile, tended to take the view that the idea was implausible. On 4 July the Belfast News Letter *commented:*

Although the prospect of such an association steering clear of politics is slender its efforts will have the good wishes of everybody who desires that better feelings should prevail between the communities in the two Irish states. As Mr J M Andrews, Minister of Finance, remarked in a speech at Castlereagh on Saturday the earnest desire of Ulster people is that North and South should rest and prosper in peace. He made it clear, however, that it is impossible to reconcile the ideal of Ulster as an integral part of the United Kingdom, loyal to the Crown and determined to maintain for the people their rights of British citizenship with the ideal of Ulster submerged in an All-Ireland republic.

As with almost any new body there were last minute doubts in the period leading up to the association's launch; Montgomery discussed this problem, which he undoubtedly saw as dithering, in his correspondence with Mary McNeill at the time.[62] In a letter to Miss McNeill on 19 October 1938 Montgomery suggested 14 December as the date on which to announce the formation of the Irish Association. On 16

November, however, in a further letter Montgomery mentioned that he had received a reply to a letter he had sent to Erskine Childers. Montgomery had passed on a copy of Childers' letter to Lord Charlemont seeking advice on whether he should meet DeValera regarding the Association. Charlemont appears to have been gravely concerned at the line Montgomery was pursuing and the General received what he described as a 'rather disconcerting document' back from Charlemont. As the launch of the Association became imminent Montgomery believed Charlemont was having second thoughts about the wisdom of launching the Association at that time. On 16 November Montgomery wrote to McNeill:

I am writing a letter of protest to Lord C, as I think he should have been more explicit in his reasons for marking time, after giving us his approval for carrying on; all this talk about 'coup d'etats', 'things behind the scenes', sounds to me rather like 'bogey-man' stuff; still, he is usually sensible enough, and there may be something in it. . . . I should be rather for putting Gough in his place; but that would weaken our case a good deal, as it would become a sort of soldiers' stunt. It is very disappointing, and personally I cannot see what harm a non-political appeal for good-will could possibly do, or how it could throw doubt on anyone's 'bona fides'. Better not show C's letter to anyone else, I think. We must just say he has ruled that we must wait a bit.

Two days later Montgomery appeared to have calmed down somewhat and took a more conciliatory attitude toward Charlemont. He wrote to McNeill:

He [Charlemont] has been for a number of years a member of a government among whom ill-will towards RCs and the South has been a principle article of faith; and therefore, for him to come into the open as President of the Association deliberately advocating goodwill in quarters where it has hitherto been regarded as out of the question, is a very bold move, which is calculated to bring on him all sorts of accusations of 'turning his coat', 'selling the pass', and all the rest of it. So I think we must be very patient with the symptoms of a certain jumpiness which are only too natural.

It is a great achievement to have converted him to our principles, and he will be a great asset if we can continue to carry him with us. Historical associations count for a great deal in this country, and it was his ancestor, aided by Grattan, who defeated the corrupt clique in Dublin 160 years ago. If I remember, there was a certain similar hesitation at that time too in his leadership of the Volunteers; but his supporters held firm and he brought it off in the end. . . . As regards Dev I think I must be guided by Lord Charlemont. I should like to see him, of course; but there are certain dangers involved, and the idea that we should 'dovetail in with' his other plans, as suggested by Erskine Childers, is I feel sure what upset Lord C so badly in his last letter.

By 18 November, after a further letter from Charlemont, Montgomery was more optimistic and in a letter to McNeill was remarkably candid about why he believed the Association needed Charlemont:

It is really Lord Ct's *name* we want for the leaflet; an ex-cabinet minister will count for more than any number of old soldiers. I don't think his subsequent help matters so much, though his political knowledge will be useful to us. I think, with care, we can keep him up to the mark; and it would be difficult to find a suitable president to take his place.

Eventually it was decided to announce the formation of the Association early in 1939. By 22 December, 1938, however, the Belfast Telegraph *had obtained a copy of the Association's pamphlet and on that date printed a brief report that 'a new effort is to be made to bring about a better feeling between Ulster and the South. What is described as an 'Irish Association' has just been formed 'to organise and give effective expression to the body of opinion known to exist among Irish people in favour of conciliation etc.' The report also named the Association's office holders. As a result of this press leak the Irish Association was pushed into releasing the pamphlet and announcing its official launch that evening.*

The pamphlet announcing the formation of the Irish Association repeated, and expanded on, the comments which Montgomery had made at the Irish Students' Congress in July. It outlined the following objectives:

This Association is for the purpose of promoting co-operation and goodwill between all sections of the Irish community. Membership will be open to all, irrespective of creed or party, who desire to promote better relations between Irish people generally.

The Association is not concerned with political or constitutional problems; its task is to make reason and goodwill take the place of passion and prejudice in determining the character of the relationships between Northern and Southern Ireland, no less than between each part of Ireland and Great Britain.

Constitutional forms are of less importance than a spirit of co-operation and friendship, and differences of opinion about the former need not prevent the growth of the latter.

The aims of the Association will be to organise and give effective expression to the body of opinion known to exist among Irish people in favour of conciliation, and to foster, through the initiative of its individual members, more neighbourly relations between Irishmen who differ from each other in politics and religion.

To encourage respect for the honest convictions with a view to discovering the best means of reconciling the economic interests of North and South.

To work for fuller co-operation in matters of general social interest.

To encourage a wider knowledge of the history, art, music and literature of Ireland.

To arrange for more social intercourse between people living in different parts of Ireland, and for meetings, lectures and conferences on subjects of common concern.

To bring home the fact that every effort to eradicate misunderstanding and disseminate good feeling in Ireland is a definite contribution to international peace and security.

To facilitate its further development the organisers require to know on what numbers an association having these aims in view will be able to count.

In an interview that evening Montgomery told the Irish News:

The Association is not in any way whatsoever to be taken as political or sectarian. It is to bring together reasonable men who would bring peace to the Irish people. For a long time they had failed to conciliate the two sections of the Irish people; and now they are going to try. If this conciliation were achieved, the constitutional problems of Eire would solve themselves. The establishment of better relations between the Six Counties and the South, between all parties and creeds, would go a long way to make other problems solve themselves. 'It is heresy to talk of two peoples in Ireland' he said. 'There is but one people in this island – the Irish people.' The intimidations carried out by sections of this community against each other must finish; these intimidations were on both sides of the Border; the blowing up of the Customs huts were an example. The people of Ireland must come together and discuss with candour the difficulties and problems of their country.

On 23 December 1938 the Irish Times *quoted DeValera as welcoming the formation of the Association by saying:*

I need only say that every effort made to promote a better understanding and to bridge difficulties between Irishmen will be welcomed by us.

The aims of the Irish Association were, from the outset, always liable to be wildly misinterpreted by those with hardline Nationalist or Unionist views; the report from the Irish News *correspondent in Dublin on 23 December for example stated:*

Such a thing as a gesture in favour of Irish reunion by prominent men who have been actively opposed to it in the past seems to the Southern mind today to be outside the region of speculation, let alone of practical politics.

The few comments which already have been heard dwell with particular interest upon the position of Sir Hubert Gough. It is not so important, perhaps, that he was the leader of the 'Curragh mutiny' in pre-war days as that during the last year or two his prestige and influence in Great Britain have been enhanced greatly by the vindication of his conduct in regard to the Fifth Army at St Quentin.

People recall that after years, during which he lived under a cloud, his vindication by Mr Lloyd-George raised him almost to the status of a popular hero, and that his views on the partition of Ireland, or on anything else, cannot fail to be heard with respect across the Channel.

It must be admitted that everybody with whom I have discussed the pronouncement is puzzled by the presence of Viscount Charlemont at the head of the signatories. Lord Charlemont is not particularly well known in the South, either personally or by repute among the people at large, and there is some speculation as to whether in the light of the pronouncement his resignation from the post of Minister of Education in Viscount Craigavon's cabinet was not due to deeper convictions than appeared upon the surface.

Sir George Franks's presence has also created interest. Sir George, of course, is well known here in Dublin, where his position as one of the heads of the British Legion in Eire frequently brings him before the public eye. He is well liked among all sections of the people, and his political views generally have been regarded as well disposed towards an enlightened nationalism, but few people would have expected to find him among the signatories of so uncompromising a statement on the desirability of unity.

The attitude of Mssrs Frank MacDermot and J J Horgan, both of whom can fairly be described as 'commonwealth men', but strongly in favour of unity, has been demonstrated on many occasions.

The Belfast News Letter *appeared to have a realistic grasp of the Association's aims and quoted Lord Charlemont as saying: 'We do not want to touch politics. Of course I cannot be responsible for the feelings of individual members, but as an association, I can assure you, that we have no interest in politics.' Charlemont referred to the fact that the title page of the pamphlet setting out the objects of the Association carried a quotation from the speech made by King George V on 22 June 1921 when he opened the first Northern Ireland Parliament: 'I appeal to all Irishmen to pause, to stretch out the hand of forbearance and conciliation, to forgive and forget, and to join in making for the land they love a new era of peace, contentment and goodwill.' Charlemont commented: 'If King George V said that I think we should also have a shot at it.'*

The Northern Whig *took a less sanguine view of the new association. On a day when the news headlines concerned the arrest and internment of 34 Belfast men as members of the IRA the newspaper's editorial noted that:*

Movements, like men, are supposed by some to be born under a lucky or an unlucky star. It would be interesting to know what the political astrologers have to say concerning the nativity and prospects of a new association brought into being to promote 'a spirit of co-operation and friendship' between Ulster and Southern Ireland. It is an unhappy coincidence that the new movement has been announced at a time when a lawless body known as the 'Irish Republican Army' is intensifying its campaign of violence and terrorism in Ulster. . . . In view of the wording of the Association's statement many Northern Ireland citizens will ask themselves how it will be possible to establish it as a cultural organisation without allowing it to become an instrument for the furtherance of 'Irish unity' in the political sense.

The Belfast Telegraph *gave a more Unionist view of the significance of the formation of the Irish Association. The newspaper reported that:*

Events have moved quickly in connection with the formation of a body styled the Irish Association, which was announced in the *Telegraph* on Thursday.

The promoters of the new organisation, whose hands had evidently been forced by the disclosure of their plans at an earlier date than they had intended, issued a printed circular last night setting forth their objects, which may be summed up in a nutshell – to bring about better relations between Northern Ireland and Eire. . . .

Representative Ulster Unionists approached on the matter today did not seem to be either concerned or perturbed about the formation of the new body, which in the words of one prominent politician was unlucky in the day its birth was announced, in that it coincided with the exposure of the IRA plot against Ulster. 'I do not see how any body like this can avoid being mixed up in politics,' said a well-known Unionist.

'The Irish question as between North and South and the
Empire is bound to involve political considerations, and I do
not think I am doing the prime movers of the Association an
injustice in saying that most of them would welcome the union
of Ireland through the abolition of the Northern Parliament.'

The Dublin press, which has always been strongly anti-
Ulster, welcomes the new movement, and it is interesting to
note that Mr DeValera has given his blessing.

1939–40
A Nationalist Critic

If Montgomery had the idea that the aims for which he and the Irish Association stood would be more readily accepted by traditional Nationalists than Unionists he would surely have been disabused of this notion by a correspondence which he conducted with Father John McShane, Parish Priest of Omagh, between August and December 1939.[63]

On 17 August Montgomery wrote in his capacity as Tyrone County Commissioner of the Boy Scouts asking Father McShane to encourage local Catholic boys to joint the Scouts. 'I need make no apology for asking for your support for a movement whose principal aim is to reduce the chance of war by encouraging those relations which make for peace' he wrote, '. . . there can be no more conclusive proof of the value of boy Scout activities than the fact that they are altogether prohibited in the Totalitarian States.' The following day McShane replied (in full) that: 'The programme as outlined in your circular is excellent. But in my opinion – which I submit subject to correction – the Scout movement from its inception, has been too closely identified with British propaganda to appeal to Irish boys.' Never one to side-step a challenge Montgomery fired off a reply in which he said:

As a student of Irish History I can quite sympathise with your point of view. In your place I should very likely say the same, and while you feel that British propaganda – I would sooner call it support of British interests – is a bar to Irish sympathy, I shall not attempt to dissuade you from keeping your boys away from the Scout movement. . . . I hope that, some day, Protestant and Catholic boys in Ireland may find it possible to meet together in the Scouts on friendly terms, as they already do in many other countries – as a matter of fact there are Scout troops in this country in which they already do so.

Having closed the discussion on the Scout movement Montgomery then launched into a discourse of wider political issues.

You and I very naturally look at the political side of the question from a somewhat different point of view: you are no doubt of pure Irish birth, as far as this is possible after the curious intermingling of races which forms such a large part of Irish History. I am of a rather Nomad race: originally Norman, then Welsh, then Scotch, and, for the last 321 years, Irish. What with this origin, and with over 40 years service in the Army I feel proud to count myself a 'British citizen', *as well as an Irishman*; much the same way that St Paul, though a genuine Jew and a native of Tarsus (no mean city), was proud of being a 'Roman citizen'. The same applies to a large extent, I think, to a majority of Ulster Protestants, as a result of the Ulster Plantation, no doubt a gross blunder on England's part at the time, but still a historical fact whose existence it is useless to try and ignore, and one for which neither present day Ulster Protestants nor the present day British government can fairly be held answerable. Cannot a fair compromise be arrived at, which would admit of people like myself remaining both Irishmen *and* British citizens? If it could, I believe the unity of Ireland would become practical politics; without it, no advance in that direction seems possible.

In the meantime what *is*, I believe, possible is a joint effort to establish better and more friendly relations between all kinds of Irishmen, and I venture to enclose a leaflet explaining the aims and policy of an association that I have been instrumental in helping to start, and which I hope you may find interesting. My feeling is that, if we could arrive at the kind of friendly atmosphere at which this association is aiming, many of the present political and constitutional problems would be found not to be so difficult after all.

McShane's reply, on 23 August, highlighted the difficulties Montgomery faced in trying to get his message across. The tone of McShane's letter was such that it might have been written by someone from a different country:

It will be obvious to you that if progress is to be made in the work of creating a better understanding among Irishmen, due attention must be paid to the viewpoint, say, of the average Paddy Murphy, whose roots are embedded in the soil of national tradition, a tradition that goes back a long, long way beyond the date of the Ulster plantation. For the moment I am not concerned with the reasonableness of Paddy's outlook. I just set down a few points of his national creed which cannot be ignored:

1 Paddy takes no pride in the British Empire. He feels no thrill when he reads of the exploits of men, even of his own race, who have helped to build up that empire. Rather his feeling is that of the dying Sarsfield when his life-blood was ebbing on the field of Landen – 'Oh, that this were for Ireland!'

2 As regards loyalty, Paddy's loyalty is to Ireland. He feels he owes the King of England the same allegiance as the Belgians did to the Kaiser during the German occupation.

3 Paddy's reading of Irish History has convinced him that for over 700 years England has been trying to make good an unjust title to rule Ireland. That claim has never been admitted. In every generation, down to our day, it has been resisted even to death. And as long as this act of aggression on the part of England continues, so long will it continue to be resisted, no matter what the cost.

4 To put the whole thing in a nutshell, Paddy is convinced that England has no right to claim ownership of a single sod of Irish earth, or a single blade of Irish grass. For over 700 years she has acted as an aggressor and until she desists from her aggression there can be no real peace between the two countries. Such being the viewpoint of Paddy Murphy down the ages, do you think it likely that he will change it today? I hardly think so. The only other alternative that I can see is for you and those of similar views to line up definitely with your own forbears of plantation stock, and, in the words of Kells Ingram – 'True men be you men, like those of Ninety-Eight.'. . . .

Yes, there is the acid test: 'If you're to Ireland true.' Let that principle be accepted, and the way is clear for union amongst

Irish-born men, if only the baneful influence of English intrigue could be eliminated.

This last matter I have mentioned constitutes the real problem. England has been very successful in applying the old Imperialistic axiom 'Divide et impera'. Only for English interference, Orange and Green would long ago have been happily blended. England wants the world to believe that Irish troubles are due to one thing alone – the inability of Irishmen to agree amongst themselves. Is not that the implication of the extract you print on the first page of the 'Irish Association' leaflet from the speech of King George V, at the opening of the Stormont Parliament on 22 June 1921? This British pose is irritating: it intensifies the bitterness between the two countries that men of goodwill wish to see removed.

Another thing that embitters our relations with England is the uninterrupted record of dishonesty of British statesmen in their dealings with us. They have never conceded a single point of Ireland's claim except in response to violence, or through fear of international complications. And when, at intervals, they were forced to make some small concession, what they gave with one hand they tried to take away with the other. . . .

The old saying about 'history repeating itself' has certainly been verified in the story of our land. In the Autumn of last year the Northern Council of Unity announced a series of meetings for the purpose of educating the British public, and also our friends on the Shankhill [sic] Road, about the evil of partition. The first meeting held in Omagh was a pronounced success. Then Stormont got alarmed and immediately an order was issued banning all similar meetings within the Six Counties. Shortly after that began the bombing campaign in England. You have no doubt seen the diagnosis of the situation made by the Hon Frank Pakenham, who was forbidden to address the students at Queen's University Belfast. 'I deplore everything connected with the bomb outbreak – but when all democratic avenues are blocked, when the elementary rights of the citizens are abrogated, when 33 men are held in gaol for an indefinite period, without charge or trial, what wonder if hotheaded, but idealistic young men grow desper-

ate, and reach the conclusion that force is the only remedy?'
You are quite right in saying that 'neither present day Ulster
Protestants, nor the present day British government can fairly
be held responsible for the Ulster plantation but I think it
would be a very easy thesis to maintain that the chief responsibility for the bombing lies at the door of No 10 Downing
Street. . . .

I feel that I owe you an apology for inflicting upon you such
a lengthy communication. My excuse is that I have been much
impressed by your evident sincerity. Hence I thought it a duty
to explain the difficulties in the way of a better understanding, first, between the representatives of the old race and the
descendants of the Ulster Planters . . . and secondly between
ourselves and England. British statesmen must face up to the
facts of the situation; they must lay aside that superiority complex when dealing with us; they must recognise that Ireland
is an ancient nation, entitled to sovereign independence, with
at least as good a title as Belgium for whom Irishmen were
asked to fight in 1914. The day that England approaches the
Irish question in this spirit, and prepares to treat with Ireland
on equal terms, then – but not till then – will the old quarrel
come to an end, and the peoples of the two countries can
settle down in friendship and harmony to cultivate the arts of
peace.

*On 28 August Montgomery replied, arguing that although
Britain's policy in the past may have been to divide and rule that was
no longer the case. In support of his argument Montgomery sent a
copy of George O'Brien's book* The Four Green Fields *to McShane
noting that O'Brien was 'a Nationalist, anti-partitionist, and a very
brilliant young professor at your National university, who puts the
point better than I can.' McShane returned the book on 7 September
(four days after Britain declared war on Germany) and in the accompanying letter wrote:*

The main point in O'Brien's book, on which you lay stress, is
contained in the sentence quoted in your last letter. 'On the
British side there can be little doubt that the British government would be only too pleased to implement any arrange-
ment providing for Irish unity *to which the Ulster Ascendancy*

would agree.' Here, we have again that irritating British pose,
referred to in my last letter, that has been poisoning all relations between the two countries, viz, that the root cause of the
trouble is the inability of Irishborn men to agree. . . . The claim
of England seems to be that a small minority in North East
Ulster, planted here by England, in the interests of England,
a minority who are content to live in Ireland, and on Ireland,
are to have the indefeasible right to dictate terms to the historic Irish nation, and in endeavouring to make good this
unjustifiable claim, can rely on the military and financial support of England. The late Bishop of Derry, a man of moderate views, once referred to this minority as 'people in whom
the natural virtue of patriotism has become perverted into loyalty to Empire.' The description is very apt.

DeValera has gone to the very utmost limit of concession in
trying to meet the prejudices of these people. The reply has
been invariably 'not an inch'. That irreconcilable attitude
would change overnight if England ceased to treat them as
pampered children, and withdrew her military and financial
support. Until that is done, experience shows that it is worse
than useless for us to make further friendly offers.

A week later Montgomery replied:

I am afraid we must agree to differ on the particular point in
question, as I agree with what George O'Brien says, and I do
not see that the arguments you put forward really prove your
case at all. . . .

Where I think you are wrong is in being in too much of a
hurry. You will probably get what you want in due course; but
'more haste less speed', and if you show too much impatience
you will probably put the clock back, as has so often happened
in Irish History before, and as has happened now as the result
of IRA activities. . . .

PS: The real point at present is that it is not the British government who maintain partition, but the Ulster Protestants
who hold the British government in a cleft stick. They say 'You,
or your predecessors put us here 300 years ago, and guaranteed our status as members of the British Empire; you cannot
honourably turn us out of that Empire now.' If Ireland would

agree to come into the Commonwealth, on condition that partition was done away with, I believe the problem could be solved.

PPS: Try coming into the war on the side of the Poles, French and English. It might work wonders.

McShane wrote to Montgomery again on 22 September noting that:

Your angle of vision on Irish affairs is far removed from mine, yet you manage to express your viewpoint in a spirit that breathes friendliness and goodwill. My method of approach is more blunt. For that there are historical reasons. We of the older race for centuries have had to sleep in our armour. This applies particularly in the North. We are like the Israelites who, in trying to rebuild the walls of their city, had to work with the trowel in one hand and the sword in the other. . . .

If I may borrow a word used by you in one of your letters, your line of argument is 'vitiated' throughout by the assumption on your part that the rights – genuine or imaginary – of an alien colony in our country, a colony who refuse to become citizens of Ireland, who persist in regarding themselves as a British garrison, are more sacred than the rights of the people in whose country they have been unjustly established, by the right of the sword, and whose constitution they refuse to recognise. You further maintain that since England has guaranteed this group of self-confessed aliens certain rights, inconsistent with the rights of the Irish nation, she is bound in honour to make good her guarantee. I wonder. In the penny catechism put into my hands as a child I find the following question and answer:

Q 'If one swears to do an unlawful thing, is he obliged to perform his oath?'
A 'No, but he is obliged to repent of having taken such an oath.'. . . .

This, I think, should be a sufficient answer to your difficulty about England being in a 'cleft-stick' on account of her unjustifiable guarantee. The landlords of other days – with some honourable exceptions – regarded themselves as a

British ascendancy garrison, whose position was guaranteed by the British Empire. When numbers of them had been shot by an outraged tenantry, England woke up, and their vested interests were bought out. The present ascendancy party will be welcome as free citizens in a free Ireland. If they refuse, let England take steps to have them bought out. The price will be high, but not too high to purchase Irish friendship. . . .

You believe that if we tried coming into the present war on the side of the Poles, French and English, it might work wonders. This seems to me an echo of what we were told in 1914. We were urged to forget our own unfinished struggle for freedom, to forget about the Broken Treaty of Limerick, and to go out to avenge the Broken Treaty guaranteeing the freedom of Belgium. This was to be a war to end all wars, a war for the freedom of small nations; and a special appeal was made to Catholic Irishmen to fight for Catholic Belgium as they are now being urged to fight for Catholic Poland. Redmond, in spite of his betrayal by the Asquith government, took up the matter with enthusiasm. But Carson was wiser in his generation. Before allowing a single one of his followers to leave the shores of Ireland, he made a hard and fast bargain. Redmond did the generous thing, and he died a broken man. Carson became a Cabinet minister.[64] His statue, in characteristic pose, now adorns the approach to the building, built by the British taxpayer, to house that assembly, miscalled a 'Parliament', in reality, owing to gerrymandering, a glorified Orange Lodge, a fitting monument to commemorate the dismemberment of this ancient nation. . . .

You say you will be seventy next year. I will be sixty-three. We are both getting on. You are rightly anxious for the promotion of friendly relations between Irishmen. On our side there is no trouble. The trouble lies with the 'not an inch' party backed up by England. What is the use of England talking platitudes about 'aggression' in certain parts of the Continent, when she herself has been an aggressor in Ireland for 700 years?

Montgomery replied on 23 September:

Your letter, which covers such a lot of ground that I really have not time to attempt to answer it fully, does not make me feel any less 'friendly', because I never can see that a difference of opinion on political questions need affect one's personal relationships, and I feel perfectly sure that if Irish people could be got to discuss the problems that divide them in a more tolerant way, admitting that there may be reason on both sides, a great many of these problems might be solved. If you will excuse my saying so, your letter is imbued with a spirit of bitterness which is bound to defeat your own cause, because you will never persuade the average Englishman, who is completely ignorant of Irish history, that either he or his leaders are as bad as you think they are. I would remind you of a saying of Edmund Burke's which was certainly true up to quite recent times, but is less true now: 'England's chief guilt lies in its total neglect, its utter oblivion, its shameful indifference, and its entire ignorance of Ireland, and of everything that relates to it and not in any oppressive disposition towards that unhappy region.'

Those in power in Ireland have always succeeded in concealing from the British public the real situation in Ireland; and unfortunately Irishmen by their ill-judged action, have been too often the involuntary means of helping them. Take this last outbreak of IRA outrages against innocent civilians, which has effectively swept away the result of all the efforts of those who have for years striven to impress British public opinion about Ireland, and were *steadily succeeding.* You people who allow bitterness to become an obsession are, in my opinion, doing infinite harm and spoiling your chances of success. At the same time I can quite sympathise with it, because it is the natural result of studying Irish history, which I have done to a considerable extent myself, during the last ten years, and I can understand what you must feel, but when you allow this obsession to warp your judgement to the extent of believing that the British sank the 'Athenia', and not being able to draw a distinction between the German action in this war and the brave defence of that gallant and long-suffering country, Poland, whose history is so similar to your own, it makes me despair of any solution of the Irish question being possible and induces me to think that the efforts I and others have been making in that direction in years past, are a pure waste of time! This is the more so because I have spent a great deal of my earlier life in England and know that the English people are most of them tolerant and broad-minded, much more so than they used to be: and that if the truth about Ireland could be brought home to them in clear and temperate language, they would be the first to see she got fair play.

It is true, of course, that in the past reforms have been extracted by violence that were denied to persuasion and the resulting conclusion drawn is a great misfortune. I am glad to see that the wiser heads in Ireland, among whom I include DeValera, no longer take that view. . . . If you compare the last agreement with anything that has happened in the past the progress is prodigious, but the situation has again been spoiled by threats. The one that has caused most uneasiness is the suggestion that if British troops were removed the Ulster question would soon be settled; that was a distinctly backward step, and if the suggestion were carried out, civil war would be much more likely to be the immediate result than settlement, with a repetition of what happened after the 1641 rising.

If you really want a settlement now, my advice would be: come into the war on the side of the allies; the impression in England and all over the Commonwealth would be overwhelming: I hope to see it! A good deal of the remainder of your letter would have found an answer if you had taken the trouble to read *The Four Green Fields* instead of returning it to me. If you like, I will send it to you again. If you have time to write a letter of this length you have time to read the book! I am afraid my time is now up; but I would like to criticise one other point. 'Repentance' means, as you say, taking steps to undo the wrong one has committed. *But not at someone else's expense* as would be the case if an unwilling Ulster were driven out of the Commonwealth against her will. Surely you can see that?

PS: You seem to me to forget or ignore the 'plantation' of Ulster. An event of that sort which happened over 300 years ago, and which still to a large extent governs the situation, cannot be removed by a stroke of the pen.

The following day Montgomery sent a further letter in which he returned The Four Green Fields *to McShane and added that although he did not agree with everything O'Brien wrote in the book he supported the book's general point of view. On 27 September Father McShane replied, asking Montgomery to read W S Armour's* Facing the Irish Question *and said:*

You appear to have got the impression that I was animated by bitterness. Not at all. I simply put down certain facts, unpalatable no doubt, but facts which cannot be controverted, and which must be taken into account by any honest man who wishes to go to the root of the trouble. My language was strong – like that of Paul of Tarsus at times – but not, I submit, intemperate. We are recommended to combine hatred of sin with love of the sinner. When dealing with oppression I try to follow the same line. . . .

Your solution seems to be: 'Let the Irish nation come into the Commonwealth, and all will be well.' What about the other alternative: 'Let the alien colony come into the Irish nation.' Now, do not accuse me of bitterness if I say that the second solution appears to me more in accordance with elementary justice. It has the additional advantage of making for real friendship between England and Ireland.

On 28 September Montgomery wrote that he had already read Armour's book several times and that he knew Armour very well personally. He continued:

I am in favour of both the solutions you mention. The first would probably bring about the second. But I do not think the second without the first is practical politics; and I am thinking, not of what may be theoretically desirable, but what may be possible.

May I suggest that to refer to Northern Ireland as an 'alien colony' is not the best way to persuade its inhabitants to come in.

On 9 October McShane wrote:

Ireland is no British colony. She has a just title to sovereign independence, a title at least as valid as that of Belgium or

Poland, or any other nation you like to mention. She cannot forget – though England has tried to make her forget it – that when Europe was sunk in barbarism, after the fall of the Western Empire, she did more than any other nation to restore Christian civilisation to Europe: that her own native civilisation, christianised in the 5th century by St Patrick, was interrupted in its development, first by Danish incursions, and again by the Anglo-Normans in 1169. The struggle that then began is still going on. By brute force and penal enactments successive British governments have endeavoured to wipe out every vestige of native culture and civilisation. Under the system of education set up by England here in the early 19th century, little school children were flogged for using the language in which St Patrick preached the gospel. . . . In view of all these things, and many more I could add, do you not think it calls for super-human restraint on our part when Lord Craigavon indulges in a stupid sneer at what he calls 'this archaic tribal tongue'. We could afford to ignore a silly remark like that, were it not for the power that Lord Craigavon wields over us so unscrupulously – a power conferred on him by England. . . .

I have put the case as plainly as I can, and, I admit, pretty strongly. But there is no earthly good in us all living in a fool's paradise. We must face facts. Peace must be based on justice, and justice must be done should the heavens fall.

You think it unwise to use the term 'alien colony'. Here let me say I would never dream of including under that caption honest, well-intentioned men holding the views you hold. I refer to the 'not an inch' party for whom Lord Craigavon speaks, who are striving might and main to stifle even discussion on a subject that is embittering relations between Irish-born men, and the relations between Ireland and England. What name are we to give them? What about 'British garrison'? They used to take pride in that name. Or perhaps 'The Ulster Ascendancy Party'? The word 'ascendancy' is surely an ugly word. It seems to imply that these people consider themselves made of a superior kind of clay, a chosen race. However, they are quite welcome to the title as far as we are concerned.

The correspondence continued in a similar vein until the end of the year, to be resumed briefly in April 1940. On 14 April McShane wrote:

I feel that the correspondence between you and me has been futile, as futile in its way as the agitation carried on in a foreign parliament by Irish representatives from Parnell to Redmond. I had to rub my eyes when, in your last letter, I found you raising – as if for the first time – points I had already disposed of in a way that would carry conviction to anyone, except one who accepted as fundamental the principle referred to by Armour: *'Ireland is always in the wrong.'* . . . .

Much as I have been interested in our exchange of views, I am afraid I must call a halt. Your viewpoint and mine are poles apart. Your idea of 'conciliation' is that the historic Irish nation, after a seven-century struggle against aggression, should calmly accept the terms laid down by the aggressor. It will not work. The aggressor must cease from aggression. Then, but not till then, can the foundation of a permanent peace, a peace based on justice, be established between the two countries. . . .

PS: Though Britain is engaged in a war to uphold the rights of 'democracy' still, if I ventured to express in public what I have written to you in private, Britain's garrison in our country would soon take steps to provide me with lodgings on the Crumlin Road.

The correspondence concluded on 18 April 1940 when Montgomery wrote to McShane saying:

I am afraid that, as you say, it will serve no useful purpose to continue our discussion further. But I should like to thank you for having put your views so candidly before me and I do not think an interchange of views is ever 'futile' so long as they are genuine on both sides. Your letters have made me realise pretty well that the point of view of what perhaps I may call, without offence, the extreme left wing of the Nationalist party, really are. I have a great deal of sympathy with those views in theory, and have read enough Irish history to understand their origins and force. Where I think we shall have to agree to differ is as regards their practical utility for the future good of Ireland, which is what I am chiefly concerned with. . . .

Well, I must, I suppose, now bid you farewell and trust that we part no worse friends as the result of a candid interchange of views.

It is worth noting, however, that a somewhat more enlightened Nationalist viewpoint was expressed a decade later by the Taoiseach, John A Costello, when he replied to a letter from Montgomery on 22 September 1949.[65]

I fully agree with your view that the problem of partition is a very complex one and that over-simplification, instead of being helpful, can be a serious hindrance to the cause of unity. I am fully satisfied that there is no easy or short cut to the end which we both desire and I have no doubt that the more knowledge of each other that our people, North and South, have, the nearer we approach to a genuine understanding of the real difficulties underlying partition. I know full well that there are many well-intentioned people in the Six Counties, but the trouble is, unfortunately, that the world hears too little of them because their reasoned and reasonable views are submerged by the loud voices of a group which has learned little and forgotten nothing and which tries to shape the future by refurbishing the catch-cries of the past.

PART II

IRELAND AND THE WAR

PAMPHLET ON IRISH AFFAIRS PUBLISHED BY
THE IRISH ASSOCIATION

Foreword

This pamphlet, the first of a series on Irish affairs to be published by the Irish Association, is an attempt to state objectively the Irish attitude to the war. It has become clear for some time, even to the politicians, that as the result of past political and religious differences the only agreement at present possible between Ireland and its six separated Northern counties, politically known as Northern Ireland, is an agreement to differ. We must learn to be good neighbours before we can be good friends. But even such an agreement is impossible unless the people on each side of the border try to understand each other's point of view. This cannot be achieved without that contact and explanation between Irishmen of all kinds which it is the principal aim of the Irish Association to provide, and which has so far been lamentably lacking. The war, whilst it has revealed the deep difference of outlook between Ireland and its separated Ulster counties, a difference the reality of which it is both foolish and dangerous to ignore or to underestimate, has also forced the British and Irish Governments to recognise the geographical and strategical unity of the whole country. No permits are required to cross the Northern border, no letters are censored between Dublin and Belfast, conscription has not been applied to Northern Ireland, and the Irish economic structure as a whole has, in spite of neutrality, been perforce adjusted to suit the war necessities of Great Britain. In fact no other course was possible and thus the fundamental unity of Ireland has been made clear. Most intelligent Irish people are also beginning to realise that the issues in this war transcend mere questions of power politics and that

Christendom is once more faced with the old challenge in a new form. It is a challenge which, in the last analysis, no Irishman, be he Protestant or Catholic, can ignore, for it imperils all he holds sacred. That our people as a whole have not so far been able to give corporate expression to this feeling is their misfortune, but not altogether their fault. If this pamphlet makes clear the present position of our divided country and the weakness which results therefrom it will have served its purpose.

March 1940

NEUTRAL IRELAND

On the Eve

In order to understand the Irish attitude towards the war one must recall the situation which existed on the eve of its commencement. For eight months previously a series of explosive outrages, preceded by an ultimatum to the British Government, had been perpetrated throughout England by the IRA. As a result much property had been destroyed and several people seriously injured, some fatally. These outrages culminated on 25 August 1939 with a bomb explosion in a Coventry street entailing the loss of five lives. To meet this threat to public order and security the British Government enacted legislation which enabled them to expel from the country persons suspected of IRA activities. All through August numerous expulsion orders were made and carried out under these powers. Mr Sean Russell, the reputed leader of the IRA who was in America ostensibly collecting funds for his campaign of outrage, stated, in an interview at Chicago on 13 August, that the number engaged in the English bombing campaign was between 500 and 1,000 members of his organisation, and expressed the belief that no concession could be obtained from England except by the use of arms. At the same time he added that the last thing they wanted to do was to take

life. The concession which the bombs were directed to secure
was apparently the evacuation of British troops from Northern Ireland.

The Irish Government, no doubt alarmed by these direct
challenges to its authority and aware that this criminal conspiracy was being directed from Ireland, issued proclamations
on 28 August putting into force those portions of the recently
enacted Offences Against the State Act which enabled them
to set up a special court for the trial of political prisoners and
also to search and intern suspected persons without trial.
When the constitution of this court was announced on 25
August it was found to consist of the same military officers as
had discharged a like duty under the Cosgrave Government
in 1931. During its terms of office for the last seven years Mr
DeValera's Government have alternately cajoled, rewarded
and threatened these terrorist elements, but they have never
resolutely faced the issue of dealing with them in a decisive
manner. They were of course seriously hampered by their own
past promises and policy. Elected on a programme which
sought to revive anti-English sentiment and led to a prolonged
dispute with Great Britain over the retention of the land annu-
ities and other moneys, they encouraged their more extreme
followers to believe that they intended to proclaim an Irish
Republic. They also developed and enlarged the centrifugal
policy of their predecessors in relation to the British Commonwealth until finally our connection with that body was
reduced to the external association arising from the recognition of the King as the channel for communication with other
countries. The settlement of the dispute with Great Britain in
April, 1938, was unfortunately not complete, as the British
Government retained its control over Northern Ireland. The
failure to achieve a complete settlement between the two Governments afforded Mr DeValera grounds for reiterated com-
plaints and an excuse for refusing to support British foreign
policy. There is no doubt that this situation not only encouraged the extremist leaders to take action in England but also
made it impossible for the Irish Government to enter the war
on the side of Great Britain. It was not until 25 August that
any official voice in Ireland indicated alarm. On that day Mr

Lemass, then Minister for Industry and Commerce, speaking at the opening of a steel mill in Cove, said that the immediate stopping of their industrial expansion might prove to be the least serious consequence if a European war broke out. The probable results for the people of Ireland appalled, he said, all who had given thought to it. They were so serious that he expressed surprise that the public mind had not yet sufficiently concerned itself about them. War, he added, would mean a period of great hardship, even if they never heard a shot fired. The virtue of discipline alone could help them and he appealed to those in a position to influence public action in all walks of life to prepare the public mind for the situation that might arise. This speech indicated clearly how little the Government themselves had expected war or prepared the people's minds for such a possibility.

NEUTRALITY

On 2 September, the day before Great Britain declared war, the Dail and Senate were hurriedly summoned to pass two emergency measures. The first amended the Constitution and enabled both Houses of Parliament by joint resolution to declare that a state of emergency existed even though Ireland was not actually at war. Both Houses on passing the Bill adopted resolutions to that effect. The second measure was an Emergency Powers Act giving the Government power by order to make such provisions as in their opinion were necessary or expedient for securing the public safety, the preservation of the state, the maintenance of public order, and the provision and control of supplies and services essential to the life of the community. When introducing these two bills in the Dail, Mr DeValera said that he did not think their policy of neutrality would come as a surprise to anybody for he had stated in the preceding February that in the event of a European war it was the aim of his Government to keep this country out of it. It was, he said, a policy which could only be pursued if they had a determined people who did not wish to injure anybody or to throw their weight on one side or the other. They, of all nations, had known what force used by a strong nation against a weaker one meant. They had known what invasion, what partition meant. They were not forgetful of their own history. As long as any part of their country was subject to force by a stronger nation, then their people, no matter what sympathies they had, should look to their own country first and consider its interests. He assured the Dail that, in the exercise of the special powers granted to them, the Government would have regard to constitutional right and practice and summon the Dail to meet as frequently as possible. Speaking the same day in the Senate, Mr DeValera intimated that the German Minister in Dublin had called on him on 31 August to inform him of Germany's peaceful attitude towards Ireland and had stated that if Germany were engaged in a European war the German Government would respect Ireland's neutrality provided that it was adhered to. Mr DeValera stated he had replied that the Irish Government wished to remain at peace with Germany as with all other powers. Whether similar communications concerning our neutrality were also made to the British Government was not disclosed.

The policy of neutrality was not challenged by anyone during the Dail debate, but Mr James Dillon, TD, the deputy leader of Fine Gael, the largest opposition party, who was the first opposition speaker, said our neutrality should not be taken as meaning that we were indifferent to the issue of the conflict. He said that he believed the vast majority of the Irish people placed their sympathy on the side of Poland, France and Great Britain against Berlin and Moscow, and he thought it right that should be placed on record. During the Senate debate some speakers expressed regret that the Irish people had not a different conception of where their interests lay but agreed that the state of public opinion made any other policy impossible. Even the *Irish Times*, which is definitely pro-British in sentiment, admitted that in all the circumstances it was the only policy the Government could pursue. But there are of course many people in Ireland who, however much they may wish loyally to accept the Government's decision, cannot be neutral in thought. The great majority of these feel that our interests economic, political and spiritual are so indissolubly bound up with those of Great Britain and France that if those powers were to go down before the onslaught of Hitlerism the future of Ireland, and indeed of European civilisation itself, would be dark indeed. Others, whilst hating Hitlerism and all its works and pomps, cannot forget the cynical dismemberment of *Czecho-Slovakia* in which Poland joined, and feel that the present war is only one more move in the game of power politics from which Ireland has everything to lose and nothing to gain. They cannot see why we should participate in this war any more than Belgium, Holland, Switzerland, or the Scandinavian countries, all of which represent the best kind of democratic community. On the other hand there is universal condemnation of Russia for its disgraceful attack on Finland, which has opened our eyes to the fact that no small nation is safe by itself in the modern world. Another point of view is held by people like Professor James Hogan, who holds the Chair of History at University College, Cork, and is an authority on the Soviet regime. In a letter to the Press immediately after the beginning of the war he said that the triumph of Germany and Russia would mean the end of Christian Europe and the inauguration of a world in which there would be no room for those values which redeem the life of man from the life of the beast. At the same time he can only, somewhat illogically, advise that whilst in no way countenancing Germany's conduct we should wait and see.

Another attitude was voiced by Cardinal MacRory, Archbishop of Armagh, in a speech at Derry on 1 October. He said it was the duty of all sincere Christians to pray fervently that the conflict might be speedily ended and be followed by a just peace. There seemed, he said, to be more hope of a just peace now than if the war were fought to a finish; for then, whichever side won, it would probably be a victor's peace sowing the seeds of future war. Moreover no Christian could contemplate calmly the prospect of Christians slaughtering one another for three or four years and thus smoothing the way for the spread of Russian Communism. He hoped and prayed no section of Irishmen would do anything in the critical times before us to endanger the peace of this country and involve us perhaps in fratricidal strife.

There remains, of course, the irreconcilable minority whose hatred of England, nourished by past wrongs, blinds them to all other considerations, and, who would, if they could, assist Germany. The recent seizure of a million rounds of ammunition from the Magazine in the Phoenix Park proves that these elements are ready and anxious to cause trouble should opportunity arise. Mr DeValera, speaking in the Dail on 29 September, described the situation fairly accurately when he said that you could divide the people here into two large classes, namely, the great bulk of the population, who, whatever may be their individual views as to its merits, desire that this country should not be involved in the war, and those who feel so strongly about the issues at stake that they wished to involve us on one side or the other. If propaganda were allowed here Mr DeValera quite accurately foresees that each element in this latter section would seek to drag us into the conflict. For this reason the Government has enforced a press censorship, which under present conditions is certainly essential. So far it has not been abused. Those who may be inclined to jibe at our neutrality would do well to remember the many thousands of Irishmen serving with the British forces. For example, nearly one-fifth of those lost in the *Courageous* bore Irish names.

WAR MEASURES

War conditions have had to take notice of the geographical and strategic unity of Ireland, for, whilst passports or travel permits are required between England and any Irish port no such restriction exists on travel between Dublin and Belfast, for the obvious reason that it would be almost impossible to close the land frontier between the North and the South. Mr DeValera's Government on 15 September arrested 93 persons suspected of activities 'prejudicial to the security of the state'. Of these 67 were permanently detained under the special powers given by the Offences Against the State Act, 1939 and 15 held for trial. During December, the High Court, however, decided that detention without trial was contrary to the provisions of the Constitution and these men were released. Subsequently the Government re-enacted the Offences Against

the State Act and the President, under the Constitution, sub-
mitted it to the Supreme Court who, by a majority, decided it
was not repugnant to the Constitution. The Civic Guard, or
police force, has also been increased by the temporary recruit-
ment of 400 men.

Immediately following the outbreak of war two new Ministries were set up, one to deal with the co-ordination of
Defence, which as we have only one defence force seems rather
absurd, and the other with supplies of essential commodities.
These new positions were assigned respectively to Mr Aiken,
the Minister for Defence and Mr Lemass, the Minister for
Industry and Commerce. Subsequent ministerial changes
made clear the paucity of first-class men in the Government
party. The obvious remedy would seem to be to call in the assistance of men of ability outside the Government party and even
outside Parliament. A plea for a government of National
Union on these lines was put forward by Mr Donal O'Sullivan,
formerly Clerk to the Senate, in which he urged that such a
government was a necessity in this time of crisis and that it
would command the maximum of co-operation. Mr
DeValera's reply to this suggestion, given during a speech in
the Senate on 4 October, was that there was something more
important than experts in government and that was to get men
with full understanding of their people. A government, he
said, who knew each other's minds and had confidence in each
other was much stronger than one whose members did not
trust each other. The only real objection to such a national
government was voiced by that veteran Nationalist Mr Henry
Harrison when he pointed out that Mr DeValera's Government is in effect a Government of the Centre and that to alter
its personnel by adding members of Mr Cosgrave's Right wing
would destroy the present position of equilibrium and be cited
as a justification for unconstitutional action by the militant
Left. It might be added that it would also probably lead to the
disruption of Mr DeValera's party.

On 8 September it was announced that the Government as
a precautionary measure had decided that it was necessary to
call up the first line of the Volunteer force, and that a recruiting campaign for the regular army would shortly be initiated.

This notice, together with the changes in the Cabinet, led to various rumours. These were dealt with by Mr DeValera when he said in the Dail on 28 September that there was no foundation for the rumour that the Government were contemplating the introduction of conscription or that there were party splits or Cabinet dissensions.

ECONOMIC PROBLEMS

On 27 September it was announced that in view of special problems arising out of the war situation in regard to their mutual trade, economic, and political relations, the Government of Ireland and the British Government had agreed that the existing system of communications between them should be supplemented by the appointment of a British representative. Sir John Maffey, a retired Indian civil servant who was later Governor-General of the Soudan and Permanent Under Secretary of State for the Colonies, has been appointed to this post. He arrived in Dublin a few days later and was cordially received by the Irish Government, who have provided suitable offices for the accommodation of himself and his staff. Up to the present Great Britain has been represented in Dublin only by a Trade Commissioner, Mr G Braddock, and, although his relations with the Irish Government and its departments have been of the most friendly and helpful character, it was essential that the wider issues which must now arise should be dealt with by a fully accredited British representative. Our peculiar position is best indicated by this title. The dominating fact that some 50% of our imports are drawn from Great Britain and some 90% of our exports are sent to that country makes it essential for agreement to be come to regarding both supply and prices. This will of course be facilitated by the fact that British buying is now organised and controlled. That there will be a strong and continuous demand for Irish agricultural produce in Great Britain during the war is certain, for the short sea journey involved and the fact that Danish supplies may be seriously reduced, if not terminated, will undoubtedly help the Irish farmers. Those engaged in the negotiations on these matters should remember that prices which do not properly remunerate the Irish farmers are not likely to yield results. At first they were much hampered by the difficulty in procuring sufficient maize and fertilisers. Without the maize our pigs cannot be properly fattened and without fertilisers increased crops will be difficult to grow. In this matter of supplies the British economic war organisation has been of great assistance. Compulsory tillage is to be enforced in future as to 12½% of all farms over ten acres in area. It is believed that next year there will be enough beet to satisfy our entire sugar requirements and enough wheat to meet half the home demand. Last year there was fortunately a bumper harvest. It is quite clear that the conditions which existed in the last war when agricultural prices soared without restriction are not likely to be repeated. There must also be considerable dislocation in our industrial plants and it will be difficult, if not impossible, to avoid serious unemployment. It has indeed already begun in the building trade through rising costs and lack of timber and other requirements. Drastic petrol restrictions which came into force on 2 October are bound to cause unemployment in the motor trade and the various motor car assembly factories.

In the Senate on 4 October, Professor Joseph Johnston, one of our economic experts, raised the question of increasing agricultural production. He said they should approach the problem in a spirit of frank collaboration with Great Britain. If they did that with the declared intention of increasing agricultural exports, they would make it easier for their neighbour to agree to the necessary imports for their industries. He thought the Government was somewhat bewildered and had not given a clear lead. They had maintained their food exports to Great Britain even when they were at war with that country in 1920–21, and they would have regarded it as a most unfriendly act if Great Britain had refused to take them. Great Britain was, he said, the national enemy only in a Pickwickian sense. The wise policy now was to use every effort to expand their agriculture and increase agricultural employment. He advocated especially an increase in the area under root and forage crops which could be used for the feeding of animals or human beings, and which would restore to the soil those

elements of fertility which the growing of other crops, especially wheat, had taken from it. There should be an immediate increase of pigs, poultry, and dairy cows and an expansion
of agricultural labour by better wages and the stoppage of work
on roads. Mr DeValera, speaking at the conclusion of the
debate, said the Government recognised their responsibilities
and did not want to shrink from them, but no government
could save the country from the results of the present world
catastrophe. They were bound to suffer and could not maintain the same standards of life as before. What was important
was to see that one section did not suffer more than another.

CONSTITUTIONAL DIFFICULTIES

Our neutrality has raised many difficulties of a constitutional nature, some of which cannot be easily resolved. For
instance, the position of Irish Minister in Berlin was vacant at
the outbreak of war, and has not since been filled. Under existing circumstances it is difficult to see how it can be if the King
remains our external representative, as His Majesty can hardly
be expected also to remain neutral. For the moment therefore the Secretary of Legation in Berlin, Mr Warnock, must
continue to look after our important interests in that capital.
Such is the lighter side of 'external association' which
apparently involves the status of a Dominion in London and
that of a neutral in Berlin. Incidentally, although the German
Minister remains in Dublin, the remainder of the German
nationals here have returned to Germany.

The sinking of the *Athenia* off our north-west coast and the
arrival of some hundreds of survivors in Galway brought us
quickly face to face with the grim realities of modern war. An
Irish branch of the International Red Cross Society has now
been established to deal with such eventualities. Some neutral
ships bound for Irish ports, although stopped by German sub-
marines, have been allowed to proceed without hindrance on
proving their destination. Several crews from torpedoed ships
have been landed on our south-west coast and on one occasion a German submarine entered Ventry Harbour, near
Dingle, County Kerry, for that purpose. One of our strategic

difficulties is that we have not, and cannot afford, a naval force capable of effectively policing our territorial waters and, if the submarine campaign is not kept under control by the British navy, serious questions may arise. A few small coastal patrol vessels have been commissioned however. The position of ships registered in Ireland and flying the national flag is also peculiar. As we have never repealed the relative sections of the Merchant Shipping Act, 1894, our ships under international law should fly the British red ensign. Moreover as the Irish tri-colour, so far as can be ascertained, has never been registered internationally, it is not to be found in any code book. It would therefore seem to have no valid existence in international law, although it has recently become the custom to fly it on ships registered in Ireland. One such ship, an oil tanker, the SS Inverliffey, flying the Irish flag, was sunk by a German sub-marine on 11 September but she was bound for a British port and her registration had been changed to British whilst she was at sea. The German submarine commander, although his attention was directed to it, refused to recognise the Irish flag. Cross-Channel sailings were also held up for a short time at the beginning of the war because the crews of some steamers refused to sail under the Irish flag unless the interests of their dependants were safeguarded. Such are the difficulties and dilemmas of neutrality and they are not likely to diminish.

NORTHERN IRELAND

Majority and Minority

The attitude of Northern Ireland to the war must be con-sidered from the majority and minority aspects, and a few out-standing facts regarding the political machinery in the area must first be noted.

The population of Northern Ireland is 1,279,745, of whom approximately 850,000 are Protestants and 430,000 are Catholics. This population is represented in the Northern Ireland House of Commons by 52 members – 39 Unionists, 2 Independent Unionists, 8 Nationalists, 1 Labour, 1 Independent Labour and 1 Independent. The Senate consists

of 26 members and is elected by the House of Commons.
Northern Ireland is also represented at Westminster by 13
members – 11 Unionists and 2 Nationalists. Unfortunately, in
the Northern Ireland House of Commons there is no adequate Opposition, as only two of the eight Nationalist members have taken their seats. At Westminster neither of the
Nationalist members attends. It should, however, be mentioned in this connection that the Nationalists do not possess
a parliamentary representation corresponding to their
numerical strength. The Northern Ireland Parliament has
control over domestic legislation subject to the jurisdiction of
the Imperial Parliament, but matters relating to peace and
war, the armed forces of the Crown, foreign relations, customs
and Inland Revenue, are reserved to the Imperial Parliament.
For military purposes, therefore, Northern Ireland is directly
controlled by the British War Office.

The Northern Government co-operates unreservedly with
the British National Government, and British regulations
regarding Food Control, ARP, etc, are carried out in Northern Ireland through the appropriate Government departments. The Unionist members from Northern Ireland in the
Imperial Parliament vote with the Government, and the majority of the Northern Ireland population has completely
adopted its policy. There is, however, no lighthearted military
enthusiasm. The war has been accepted as an inevitable evil –
the only way of combating aggression, and as a whole the
people of Northern Ireland have sincerely undertaken their
share in the gigantic struggle. The old attachment to the
Empire is so strong that, without perhaps realising the new
implications that that attachment now involves, the Protestant
majority in the Six Counties has ranged itself unquestioningly
on England's side. The Catholic section, following the strong
lead given by the Vatican, finds that all its sympathies are on
the side of democratic government against the totalitarian
conception of the State, that is to say it supports France and
Britain for moral rather than patriotic reasons. This distinction of attitude must be remembered. As in Great Britain, voluntary service of all kinds has been undertaken, work parties
are in full swing, large private houses have been offered for

hospital purposes, and industry in Northern Ireland is participating in the general output of war material, notably of ships and linen. Petrol rationing, food control, increased agricultural activity operate as in England, black-out conditions are very severe, and plans have been made for the evacuation of all school and pre-school children from Belfast should the necessity arise. It remains, however, true that the daily life of the Six Counties has not been dislocated as in England. This is chiefly due to the fact that conscription is not applicable to Northern Ireland, which necessitates in turn a fuller consideration of the attitude of the minority, and of events which took place before the outbreak of war. It must be recognised that in Northern Ireland political parties unfortunately coincide with religious groupings. To all intents and purposes the Unionist majority corresponds to the Protestant population and the Nationalist minority to the Catholic population; there are, of course, some notable exceptions to this rule, but broadly speaking it holds good.

THE STRUGGLE AGAINST CONSCRIPTION

With the steadily deteriorating international situation the possibility of the necessity of some form of conscription was evident in England by April 1939, and the position of Northern Ireland became at once a vital question. As Compulsory Service was part of the whole question of defence the issue lay entirely with the Imperial Parliament, and from the first mention of the proposed innovation the majority in Northern Ireland was prepared to accept whatever regulations were imposed in Great Britain, as the logical outcome of the existing political relationship. Not so the Nationalist minority; their violent opposition was at once publicly declared. Meetings were held, speeches were made, and resolutions were adopted against any form of compulsory military service being applied to the Six Counties. From the beginning of this campaign the Nationalist minority here looked to Mr DeValera, Prime Minister of Eire, as their leader and protagonist. As only two of the Nationalist members sit in the Northern Parliament, no adequate opinion could be voiced there, and in any case, the

matter was beyond the authority of that body. At Westminster
where the issue would be determined, the minority, owing to
its own action, was completely unrepresented. The grounds
on which this strong opposition was mobilised were that the
first allegiance of Irish Nationalists was to the Irish Nation
alone, and that Compulsory Military Service was being forced
on a part of Ireland by an outside power, namely England,
which had no right to do so.

At a Conference of Northern Nationalists held in Belfast on
27 April, Mr DeValera was called upon to inaugurate an all-
Ireland movement to resist the imposition of conscription in
the North, and on the following day a manifesto was sent to
him from Derry denying 'the right of any foreign country to
conscript the manhood of this country or any part of it, and
repudiating the statement of Lord Craigavon that the people
of Ulster desire to be included in the Conscription Act, as he
could not speak for 500,000 of the people of the Six Counties,
and the failure of the British National Service Scheme proved
that in this the so-called loyalists were not behind him.' The
Northern Ireland Labour Party also protested against conscription, but on the grounds expressed by the Labour Party
in England.

Meanwhile the attitude of the Unionist majority was being
voiced by Lord Craigavon. On 25 April he issued the following statement to *The Belfast News-Letter* – 'We as part of the
United Kingdom would naturally fall into line with the rest of
the country. In the case of defence and war these are matters
for the United Kingdom as a whole,' and two days later the
political correspondent of that paper declared that 'the decision of the British Cabinet on the question whether or not the
Compulsory Service Bill shall apply to Ulster is awaited with
keen interest. In the lobby there was keen speculation, some
members inclined to the view that the Bill would be applied
automatically to Northern Ireland, if conscription was considered necessary in the national interest then they would
accept it. Nationalists, of course, would oppose conscription
vigorously. . . . In business circles I found that there was almost
unanimous support for compulsory service.' Nevertheless, the
absence of other than purely parliamentary support was

noticeable. While the Nationalist minority was publicly pledging itself to resist conscription there is no recorded evidence that the organisations of the majority, such as Orange Lodges, Unionist Associations, and so forth, threw in their weight with equal force to support it: Lord Craigavon's assurances appeared to be considered sufficient.

On 26 April Mr Chamberlain announced at Westminster that a Bill for Compulsory Service would be introduced, but the position of Northern Ireland was not mentioned. The following day Lord Craigavon communicated to the British Government 'that Ulster, as a most loyal part of the United Kingdom would deeply resent any suggestion that she should not be included in the Military Training Bill. . . . He pointed out that any alternative would be regarded as a slight by the people of Ulster and concluded by emphasising the ardent desire of the people of Ulster to be called upon to bear the same obligations as their fellow citizens in the rest of the United Kingdom, and expressed the hope that the British Government would make no reservations whatever in the application of the measure to Northern Ireland.' On the same day Mr DeValera cancelled his visit to the United States, and it is understood that strong warnings were sent to Mr Chamberlain by Mr DeValera, through the High Commissioner of Eire in London, to the effect 'that the application of the Conscription Bill to the Six Counties would have an effect almost approaching civil conflict in the North. The introduction of conscription to any part of Ireland would be considered as a grave blow to Anglo-Irish friendship.'

Furthermore, on 29 April the Cardinal Archbishop of Armagh, The Most Rev Dr MacRory, together with the Bishops whose dioceses lay wholly or partly in Northern Ireland, issued the following statement – 'In view of the anxiety that exists at present among our people on account of the rumours of conscription, we deem it a solemn duty to make known our considered judgement on the situation that confronts us in the Six Counties. We are convinced that any attempt to impose conscription here would be disastrous. Our people have been already subjected to the gravest injustice in being cut off from one of the oldest nations in Europe, and in being deprived of their fundamental rights as citizens in their own land. In such circumstances to compel them to fight for their oppressors would be likely to rouse them to indignation and resistance.'

'It would be regarded by Irishmen not only in the Six Counties but in Eire and throughout the world wherever they are found as an outrage on the national feeling and an aggression upon our national rights. If those who think they have benefited by Partition desire to show their gratitude it should not be necessary to impose upon them compulsory military service. In actual fact the British Government stands to lose rather than gain by such an attempt.' These sentiments were further emphasised by the Cardinal in a public utterance next day.

On 1 May the Belfast Trades Union Council sent the following telegram to Mr Chamberlain 'viewing with concern the introduction of conscription by the National Government . . . they called upon the people to offer the strongest possible resistance to any attempt that was likely to be made to have conscription imposed.'

When the text of the Bill appeared on 1 May, Northern Ireland and the Isle of Man were found to be excluded from its provisions, but power was given to the King by an Order in Council to direct that the Act might be applied to those areas 'with such modification and adaptation as may be specified in the Order.'

The next day Lord Craigavon had an audience with Mr Chamberlain: he left Ulster 'hoping, expecting, believing that there will be no differentiation between His Majesty's loyal subjects in Northern Ireland and elsewhere.' But more protests followed. Mr DeValera contended that if a plebiscite were taken four out of the six counties would vote for inclusion in Eire. Lord Craigavon continued to press for the inclusion of Ulster. He placed the whole resources of the Province at the disposal of the Imperial Government, and asked to be informed in what way Ulster could best serve 'the mother country'. On his return from London he stated that he was entirely satisfied with his visit, and that it was for the Imperial Government to come to a decision on Ulster's most generous gesture.

When the Bill was read a second time Mr Chamberlain

declared it would not apply to Northern Ireland. He alluded to his interview with Lord Craigavon and to the loyalty of the people of Northern Ireland. 'Nothing,' he said 'would arouse so much resentment in Ulster as the suggestion that they wished in any way to be relieved of the burdens borne by their fellow citizens over here.' On the other hand Mr Chamberlain said that Lord Craigavon had agreed that 'nothing should stand in the way of the unity of the country in this matter and that nothing should happen that could be exploited by people not friendly to ourselves. The attitude of Lord Craigavon was warmly appreciated by the British Government.' Mr Chamberlain added that in addition to the existing voluntary units in Northern Ireland it had been decided to reconstitute the North Irish Horse as a light Tank Unit of the Royal Armoured Corps. The amendment to the Bill excluding Northern Ireland from compulsory service was vigorously opposed by the Unionist members for Northern Ireland at Westminster.

Lord Craigavon said in the Northern Ireland House of Commons on 4 May – 'Loyalty as we understand it in Ulster . . . means supporting the Government of the United Kingdom in the heroic task that they are undertaking. If we did otherwise the high esteem in which we are held in Great Britain and the Empire might be vitally prejudiced. . . . As in the past our loyalty is not conditional in any way, and our people can best contribute in these difficult times to assist the mother country by an unquestioning acceptance of whatever decision the British Government may find it necessary to make.'

On the same day a conference of Nationalist members of both Houses of the Northern Parliament passed a resolution expressing their sincere gratitude to Mr DeValera for his swift response to their request to assist them in opposing conscription, and their profound appreciation of the timely declaration of the Cardinal and Bishops.

And so this dangerous question was settled.

When considering the attitude of the Nationalist minority it should be remembered that the opposition to conscription was not due to pro-Nazi sympathies but to the intention to resist what was considered to be a grave imposition on Irishmen by the British Parliament.

This detailed account of the struggle in Northern Ireland regarding conscription is necessary if the outlook of the majority and the minority since the outbreak of war is to be appreciated.

SINCE THE OUTBREAK OF WAR

The attitude of the majority has naturally been one of complete support of British policy. Foreign affairs, and the issues of peace and war, are excluded from the purview of the Government of Northern Ireland, but behind the necessary official acceptance of the policy of Great Britain there is whole-hearted sympathy and support for the cause which she is championing, or rather a complete identification of interest. The Labour Party has adopted the attitude of their colleagues in Great Britain.

The minority has shown no sign whatever of changing or regretting its policy with regard to conscription. Writing on 4 September of the outbreak of war and of the suffering and distress already incurred, the Nationalist organ *The Irish News* said – 'Unfortunately here in North East Ulster that suffering cannot be faced by a united people; the position makes that impossible, a position for which Britain herself cannot escape responsibility. 'So long as a part of Ireland is subject to force by a stronger nation, it is only natural that the people should look to their own country first,' said Mr DeValera in the Dail on Saturday. However awkward it may be that sentiment finds an echo in the hearts of many here. It is felt stronger perhaps because of the fact that those imbued with it are cut off from the Motherland.' The following day the same paper declared 'that in the circumstances it is but natural that the public should strive to do what they can, not merely to keep calm and resolute, but to work for the protection of the community as a whole in the critical days that lie ahead,' and while maintaining, officially, a neutral attitude towards the British Government all sections of the Catholic population have taken part in ARP, and National Service; all are facing food rationing, the possibility of evacuation and other war emergencies without complaint; and farmers of every religious persuasion and political creed are ploughing the land and bearing with both grumbling and fortitude, the shortage of feeding stuffs.

It is true that in the first week of war gas masks were publicly burnt and streets and houses illuminated in the Nationalist area of Belfast, and that, in retaliation, Catholic workmen were turned out of the shipyards; but the influence of the IRA is responsible for the one outrage and excited extremists of the Unionist side for the other. The workmen were reinstated after a week, the Nationalist district is now as dark as any other area of the city, and such incidents have not been repeated.

Figures for recruiting in Northern Ireland since the outbreak of war are not available for publication, but it is safe to say that neither the Catholic Church nor the Nationalist party have made any pronouncement against voluntary enlistment, and that the Catholic population provides a substantial share of the recruits from Northern Ireland.

Without doubt the German–Soviet Pact, the destruction of Poland, the outrageous attack on Finland, and the attitude of the Papacy to the international situation, have had a profound influence on the view of the minority in Northern Ireland. The Catholic Church knows that the allied countries are fighting the Church's deadly foes, and while the Catholic population in Northern Ireland has not (with some exceptions) identified itself with Britain, their whole sympathy must inevitably be with the Allied cause. Cardinal MacRory speaking in Derry on 1 October, after deploring the war, and pleading for peace negotiations went on to say 'I hope and pray that no section of Irishmen, north or south will do anything in these critical times before us to endanger the peace of our country and involve us perhaps in fratricidal strife.' Nevertheless, having regard to the international situation and its bearing on the doctrine of the Catholic Church, some people in Ireland find it hard to understand the statement of the Irish Hierarchy made on 10 October, which while expressing deep sympathy for Poland, horror of modern warfare and the need for the practice of Christian virtues goes on to say 'the greater part of our country, we regret not all, is not directly involved in the conflict.'

In conclusion the opinion voiced by the Eire correspondent

to *The Times* on 4 November, may be quoted: 'Probably for the first time in history the British and Irish peoples are in complete ideological concord.' This would seem to be not only a fair statement of the present situation, but possibly, if we could but realise it, the foundation on which the future of Anglo-Irish relationship may be built, and Ireland's contribution to a new world order eventually made. For the issues which confront us transcend and should obliterate the differences which have divided the people of Ireland.

APPENDIX A

Spender Papers (PRONI D.1295/24)

Letter from General Hugh Montgomery to Spender, 9 April 1940

My dear Spender

Thanks very much for your letter. No, it wasn't Crozier, about whom I hold much the same opinion as you do!

The source of the admission about Lord Carson was Sir Chartres Biron's book of recollections, entitled *Without Prejudice*, published in 1936 by Faber and Faber.

If you will get hold of this, and turn to p 215, near the bottom, you will find the following:

'Long after,' (he had been referring to 1922), 'I was sitting next to Carson at dinner; we were talking in a friendly way about politics, and suddenly, to my astonishment, he said with every appearance of conviction; 'Well, looking back at politics, I think we made a great mistake in not accepting Mr Gladstone's first Home Rule Bill.'[1]

'I looked at him with amazement but there was no doubt about his sincerity. His belated conversion was right.'

Biron was, it is true, a political opponent of Carson's; but he was also a very distinguished and highly respected County Court Judge for 30 years, for half of that time at Bow Street, and I find it difficult to believe that he made a mistake on a matter of that sort. Unfortunately Biron died the other day; so there is no way of obtaining verification or denial from him.

Is it not possible that he might, in a confidential moment, admit to another elderly lawyer, a change of mind, which, if made generally known at that time, when the Home Rule controversy was over and done with, could have done no good, and might have had a very upsetting effect all round?

Personally, I was just as surprised as you were when my attention was just drawn to it; but after reading Hammond's admirable book on 'Gladstone and the Irish Nation' I was less so.

Best wishes, Yours ever, (Sgd) Hugh Montgomery.

Appendix A

[1] Montgomery or Biron may well have been deceiving himself here. Montgomery Hydes' *Carson* (London), pp 490–1, records in detail Carson's views of 1933; here Carson declares that Gladstone's adoption of Home Rule in 1886 made the Irish question, in effect, insoluble. Carson wrote to the historian, Sir John Marriott on 6 November 1933: 'I have never had the slightest doubt that it would have been impossible to have made any lasting settlement in Ireland after the G.O.M. had adopted the Home Rule policy, and everything that happens from day to day convinces me more and more that all the elements that had the real power were not only anti-English but are really far from being civilised. London, pp 490–491. A full reading of Biron's text reveals that he did not keep a diary and so relied on memory for these anecdotes. Biron also had a less than nuanced understanding of the complexities of Irish unionism.

THE IRISH ASSOCIATION

APPLICATION FORM

To MAJOR-GENERAL HUGH MONTGOMERY,
BLESSINGBOURNE,
FIVEMILETOWN,
CO. TYRONE.
N. IRELAND.

Dear Sir,

I wish to apply for membership of the Irish Association.

I enclose £   :   :   *

Yours faithfully,

(Signature)...

NAME AND ADDRESS (BLOCK CAPITALS).

....

....

* Subscriptions—minimum, 2/6 for Annual Members and £2.2.0 for Life Members.

THE IRISH ASSOCIATION has been formed for the purpose of promoting co-operation and mutual good will between all sections of the Irish community. Membership is open to all, irrespective of party or of religious belief, who desire to promote better relations between the Irish people generally.

The Association is not concerned with political or constitutional problems; its task is to make reason and good will take the place of passion and prejudice in determining the character of the relationship between North and South, no less than between each part of Ireland and Great Britain. Constitutional forms are of less importance than a spirit of co-operation and friendship, and differences of opinion about the former need not prevent the growth of the latter.

THE AIMS OF THE ASSOCIATION are:—

(a) To organize and give effective expression to the body of opinion known to exist among Irish people in favour of conciliation, and to foster, through the initiative of its individual members, more neighbourly relations between Irishmen who differ from each other in politics and religion.

(b) To encourage respect for the honest convictions of others, and to expose and discountenance misrepresentation, intolerance and intimidation.

(c) To study business and commercial relations with a view to discovering the best means of reconciling the economic interests of North and South.

(d) To work for fuller co-operation in matters of general social interest.

(e) To encourage a wider knowledge of the history, art, music, and literature of Ireland.

(f) To arrange for more social intercourse between people living in different parts of Ireland, and for meetings, lectures, and conferences on subjects of common concern.

(g) To bring home the fact that every effort to eradicate misunderstanding and disseminate good feeling in Ireland is a definite contribution to international peace and security.

PRINTED BY
PAPER AND PRINTING PRODUCTS LTD.,
92–97 LR. SEAN MACDERMOTT ST.,
DUBLIN.

THE IRISH ASSOCIATION TODAY

The Irish Association for Cultural, Economic and Social Relations

Founded in 1938 by Major General Hugh Montgomery and a number of associates, from both Unionist and Nationalist backgrounds, the Irish Association has from its earliest days sought to promote communication, understanding and co-operation between North and South, Unionist and Nationalist, Protestant and Catholic.

In recent years the Association has had to adapt and develop to meet new needs and challenges and also to complement rather than compete with other newer organisations also working in the area of promoting better North–South relations.

The Association's original aims remain its raison d'etre. It has, however, greatly intensified its programme of activities as it strives for greater communication, understanding and co-operation between all the peoples of Ireland.

Political Dialogue

Since 1969 the Irish Association has had to confront the need for real and continuing political dialogue. Its non-partisan stance and membership has gradually enabled it to draw into serious dialogue, and on the most contentious issues, all parties and individuals engaged in constitutional politics. This dialogue has properly involved the politicians not only with one another but with the public, North and South, as well. Only an informed public can give the politicians the freedom and support they need. These dialogues are clearly still necessary.

Cultural, Economic and Social Relations

Political discussions must always be in context, be that context cultural or religious, social or economic. Through its conferences, seminars and public lectures and its sponsorship of concerts and exhibitions, of plays and poetry readings, the Association exposes and examines the diverse contexts of Irish political divisions.

What They Said

'The Irish Association of which I was an active member for over twenty years, is a very effective contributor to the cause of Irish understanding, peace and reconciliation.'

MARY ROBINSON
UACHTARAN NA hEIREANN

'Today, more than ever, the building of trust between all the people of the island of Ireland – for which the Irish Association works so hard – is a critical need.'

CHARLES HAUGHEY

'While distrust, misinformation and ignorance dominate relations between the two political entities on the island of Ireland the Irish Association has a vital role to fulfill by promoting understanding, mutual respect and a frank exchange of views'

KEN MAGINNIS MP

'By providing for the expression and exchange of so many different perspectives on society and culture, the Irish Association adds to all our understanding. Such understanding makes an invaluable, if sometimes invisible, contribution to accommodation, reconciliation and so to peace.'

JOHN HUME MEP

'As a longstanding member of the Irish Association for many years I believe that it has a very significant role in fostering dialogue and understanding between Irish people, North and South.'

GARRET FITZGERALD, TD

Notable Recent Events

The lectures, seminars and other events set out below are a selection from the extensive programme carried out by the Association in recent years.

The Role of the Churches
Cardinal O'Fiach and Archbishop Eames

Who Speaks to Whom: Promoting Political Dialogue:
Austin Currie and Sammy Wilson

Beyond Violence
Ex-paramilitaries Shane Paul O'Doherty and Gusty Spence

History Conference for Sixth Formers from North and South

Articles 2 and 3 after the Supreme Court Judgement in the McGimpsey Case
Chris McGimpsey, Jack Lynch

A Divided Ireland in a United Europe
John Hume and Jim Nicholson with other MEP's from Ireland and the UK

The Unionist Mind and the Nationalist Mind
Dr Anthony Clare interviews Raymond Ferguson and Tim Pat Coogan

How to Commemorate 1916
A seminar with Professor Joe Lee, Dermot Ahern TD and David Trimble MP

Transport Infrastructure North and South
A conference on road and rail links

The Birmingham Six and the Media. The Lessons
Roger Bolton (Thames TV), Joe Mulholland (RTE) and Dr Mary Cullen

New Discriminations
Joint seminar with British Irish Association in Belfast

Officers

President
Professor Paul Bew, Belfast

Vice-Presidents
Dr John Bowman, Dublin
Dr Bernard Cullen, Belfast

Honorary Secretary
George Woodman, Belfast
Director
Barbara Sweetman FitzGerald

Development Committee
Gerald P. Dempsey (Chair)
Paul Bew, William Carson, Brian Garrett
Enda McDonagh, A. S. J. O'Neill
Barbara Sweetman FitzGerald

Past Presidents
1938–1946
The Rt. Hon. The Lord Charlemont PC (NI)
1946–1954
Professor Joseph Johnston FTCD
1954–1963
Sir Graham Larmor
1963–1966
J. F. Dempsey B. Comm., LLD FCA
1967–1970
Martin Wallace M.A.
1970–1973
Edmond Grace FCA
1973–1976
William Marshall
1976–1978
Donal Barrington SC
1978–1980
A. S. J. O'Neill
1980–1982
Senator Trevor West
1982–1984
Lewis Semple
1984–1986
Una O'Higgins O'Malley
1986–1988
Brian Garrett
1988–1991
Professor Enda McDonagh

NOTES AND REFERENCES

INTRODUCTION

[1] For this speech and its context see Paul Bew, *C S Parnell*, Dublin 1991, 2nd edition, pp 127–131.

[2] J Bardon, *A History of Ulster*, Belfast 1992, pp 538–539. We are indebted also to Jonathan Bardon's discussion of the 1935 riots.

[3] Statement by former President Trevor West, later Senator Trevor West and Lewis Semple, *Northern Whig*, 23 January 1954.

[4] PRONI D627/A/3/3/1–9.

[5] Mary McNeill was Hon. Secretary, Northern Committee, 1938–53, *The beginnings of the Irish Association for cultural, economic and social relations*, printed 1982, p 4. For more family context, see P Buckland, ed, *Irish Unionism 1885–1923*, Belfast 1973, pp 424–426. For the plantation, see J M Hills, 'The Origins of the Scottish Plantations in Ulster to 1625: A Re-interpretation', *Journal of British Studies*, January 1993, vol 32, pp 24–43.

[6] 'Ulster's Forgotten Gentry', *Sunday Telegraph*, 7 January 1993.

[7] *Belfast Telegraph*, 30 August 1949.

[8] Mary Harris, *The Catholic Church and the Foundation of the Northern Irish State*, unpublished Cambridge PhD thesis, 1991, p 230.

[9] P Buckland, *Factory of Grievances*, Dublin 1979, p 246.

[10] Harris, *op cit*, p 266.

[11] Harris, *op cit*, p 269.

[12] *Belfast Telegraph*, 30 August 1949.

[13] Peter Semple, *Wilfrid Bliss Spender 1912–1985: A Question of Principle*, unpublished MSSc thesis, QUB 1993.

[14] H Montgomery, *The New Northman*, vol V, no 2, 1937. See also Greta Jones, "Marie Stopes in Ireland – The Mothers' Clinic in Belfast 1936–1947", *Social History of Medicine*, vol 5, no 2, 1992. p 262.

[15] Frank MacDermot, Irish Senator, former TD of the Centre Party. Unsuccessfully contested West Belfast as a Nationalist in 1929. For his suggestive intervention in the debate on the 1937 Irish Constitution, see Angela Clifford, *The Constitutional History of Eire/Ireland*, Belfast 1985, pp. 120–3.

[16] John Joseph Horgan 1881–1967. Solicitor. Coroner for County Cork from 1914. Conducted the inquest into the victims of the Lusitania in 1915. Director of several companies, author of numerous articles: son-in-law of Bertram Windle, the liberal Catholic academic.

[17] Other early members of the Irish Association included: the author Edith Somerville; Major Leonard Darwin (son of Charles Darwin), Liberal Unionist MP for Lichfield 1892-1895 and President of the Royal Geographical Society 1908–1911; and academics J C Beckett and R B McDowell.

[18] Montgomery to Donal O'Sullivan, 3 November 1942, PRONI D2661/C.

[19] For this exchange see *Belfast Telegraph*, 1 January 1991, Brian Faulkner is probably making reference to Barritt and Carter's *The Northern Ireland Problem*, Oxford 1962, a judicious and fair work. Ironically Sir Charles Carter's evidence (21 September 1983) to the Forum Report of 1983 is a most potent critique of Nationalist assumptions on the economics of Irish unification.

[20] For this material see Andrew Gailey's forthcoming edition of the Sayers papers.

[21] The letters are now in PRONI D2661/C. In 1962 they were at Blessingbourne. Their owner, the late Captain Peter Montgomery, gave permission for their use in the lecture as did Lady Charlemont.

[22] Richard Dunphy, *The Making of Fianna Fail Power in Ireland*, forthcoming. For DeValera's thinking, see John Bowman, *De Valera and the Ulster Question*, Oxford 1983, a superb study.

[23] Gareth Griffith, *Socialism and Superior Brains: The Political Thought of Bernard Shaw*, London 1993, pp 214–215.

[24] Mary McNeill to her sister Peg, 4 April 1938. These quotations are from the Mary McNeill letters currently in possession of Rev. Eric Gallagher.

[25] *Ibid*, 29 January 1950.

PART I

[1] There is an interesting echo to this point. In 1937 General Montgomery publicly argued that some form of Irish unity on a dominion basis was essential to British security in the event of a second world war. Only then would the stand of Ireland present no threat to Great Britain. Sir Wilfrid Spender, head of the NICS, was genuinely perturbed. Spender had sacrificed a potentially glittering career in the British army to serve Ulster Unionism; this was principally because he felt that the Asquith government's home rule policy ignored vital considerations of imperial security. Now he found Montgomery turning this argument on its head and employing it against the government of Northern Ireland. Spender felt it necessary to reply to Montgomery, whose pro-imperial credentials he fully accepted. Spender stressed, inaccurately, the alleged leftward trend in the 26 counties. This was precisely at the moment when the radicalism, such as it was, of the Fianna Fail government began to ebb. On 2 November 1937 Spender wrote: 'If the news which reaches me from the Free State is true that communism is gaining ground every day and that both

the church and the more conservative leaders are losing ground, I do not
think that even the sacrificing of Northern Ireland and the creation of
an Irish Dominion would ultimately result in the strengthening of the
British Empire.' More interestingly, Spender reiterated precisely the point
made by Charlemont earlier in his correspondence with Montgomery: 'I
am strongly concerned that the Ulster working classes appreciate the
benefits of the British connection, but if this were severed, a large proportion of those resident in Northern Ireland would change to socialis-
tic tendencies.' (PRONI D 715) For a recent attempt to recreate the
oppositional Labour culture of the entire war era, see J Keenan (ed), *The
Labour Opposition*, Belfast 1992. Ironically, these questions were to be
settled elsewhere by others and on an entirely different basis. As Professor
Cornelius O'Leary has recently suggested, the British believed that the
DeValera government turned down the British offer of Irish unity of 1940
because they felt that the Germans would dictate the terms of the peace.
On 7 July 1940 Neville Chamberlain wrote to his sister Ida: 'The real basic
fact is that it is not Partition which stands in the way at this moment but
the fear of Dev and his friends that we shall be beaten. They don't want
to be on the losing side and if that is unheroic one can only say that it is
very much the attitude of the world from the USA to Romania and from
Japan to Ireland.' (*Irish News*, 29 June 1992).

[2] Mervyn Knox-Browne, Aughentaine Castle, Fivemiletown. A Unionist
member of Clogher District Council.

[3] See, on precisely this point, *The Autobiography of Terence O'Neill*,
London 1972, p 13, which recalls the moment in 1922 when, following a
Sinn Fein inspired fire at Shane's Castle, Lord O'Neill's estate, the
Catholic head forester refused to ring the fire bell.

[4] John McGonigal KC, 1870–1943. Educated St Malachy's College Belfast,
The French College and Blackrock, Dublin. Called to the Irish Bar 1892.
Professor of the Law of Property at King's Inn, Dublin 1910–1913. Called
to the Inner Bar 1911. Senior Crown Prosecutor for the City of Belfast
1917. County Court Judge of Tyrone from 1939.

[5] Charlemont is wrong here, Wyse was a Southerner but Denis Henry hailed
from Draperstown. Wyse was Permanent Secretary at the Ministry of Education. Dr Mary Harris writes on Wyse: 'There were different types of
Catholics. Wyse had been educated at Downside and the University of
London and was frequently denounced in the *Catholic Bulletin*'. Wyse was
also a descendant of Thomas Wyse, the progressive advocate of mixed
education in the nineteenth century. See Angela Clifford, *Godless Colleges
and Mixed Education in Ireland*, Belfast 1992, pp 4–16. Henry, who was a
friend of both Craig and Carson, became a convinced Unionist as early
as the 1880s; indeed, he was later Unionist MP for Derry (1916–1921)
and then, to his death in 1926, Lord Chief Justice of Northern Ireland.
See A D MacDonnell, '*The 1918 General Election in Ulster, and a biography
of a candidate, D Henry*', unpublished, Queen's University Belfast, PhD thesis, pp 356–464.

[6] Joseph Devlin, 1871–1934. Born Belfast. Educated Christian Brothers, Belfast. Worked in Kelly's Cellars public house in Belfast as a barman before becoming a journalist and working for the *Irish News* and *Freeman's Journal*. Became Secretary of the Belfast Young Ireland Society and subsequently took up a post at the party headquarters in Dublin. As Secretary of the United Irish League he met Irish-American nationalists on visits to the USA. Became MP for North Kilkenny (1902–1906) after an unopposed by-election and subsequently won and held West Belfast 1906–1918. Instrumental in refounding the Ancient Order of Hibernians which he used as a political machine: on this account bitterly denounced by prominent nationalist William O'Brien MP as a violent manipulator who made a Catholic conspiracy the controlling force of nationalist politics. See Paul Bew, *Conflict and Conciliation in Ireland 1890–1910*, Oxford 1987. Helped organise the Irish National Volunteers in 1913 but did not support the 1916 rising. Refused to accept leadership of the Irish Party on Redmond's death and stayed close to his grass-roots support. Won Falls Division of Belfast 1918, defeating DeValera.

Nationalist MP elected for both West Belfast and Antrim in the 1921 Stormont election. Subsequently elected for West Belfast in 1925 and Central Belfast from 1929 until his death in 1934. At Stormont pursued a policy of partial abstentionism attending only when it was felt that the vital interests of Catholics were at stake. Campaigned for the maintenance of Catholic education in Northern Ireland and (unsuccessfully) supported the continuation of proportional representation in Northern Ireland elections. Elected to Westminster for Fermanagh and Tyrone in 1929 and 1931. Charlemont's verdict seems to be a harsh one, which is not to say that Devlin was a statesman. In his Westminster period Devlin was a widely respected figure in the House of Commons. It is, however, an enormously complex and chequered career currently the subject of ongoing scholarly biography by Professor A C Hepburn of the University of Sunderland. See, for example, the remarkable impression Devlin made on the Labour MP, G Barnes, *From Workshop to War Cabinet*, London 1923. Praise was heaped on Devlin by Sir Patrick Mayhew in his speech at Coleraine in December 1992; obviously Sir Patrick's speech writers were blissfully unaware of William O'Brien's charges.

[7] Thomas Joseph Campbell KC. Died 1946. Born Belfast. Educated Christian Brothers School and St Malachy's, Belfast. Editor *Irish News* 1895–1906. Called to the Irish Bar 1900, English Bar 1904. Irish Parliamentary Party candidate for South Monaghan 1918. First Treasurer of the Bar of Northern Ireland. First Nationalist Senator to sign the Roll of the Senate of Northern Ireland, 1929. Resigned from Senate 1934. Nationalist MP for Central Belfast at Stormont (in succession to Joe Devlin) from 1934 to 1946 when he resigned to become a County Court Judge. Stood for West Belfast in United Kingdom General Election of 1931 but defeated by Unionist. For an excellent recent analysis of this intensely reserved and religious man – based in part on private papers – see Philip Leonard's dis-

sertation '*T J Campbell*', MSSc dissertation, Queen's University, Belfast 1992. See Leonard's discussion of Campbell's contribution to educational debates, *NI Hansard*, vol 17, col 1278. In November 1992 Campbell's aspiration (100% grant) became official government policy.

[8] Charlemont's point about the scale of the disturbances may be a fair one but he is ignoring a vital dimension here – perhaps because he did not know the full facts. It appears from the Government files that following these attacks, the Minister of Home Affairs, R Dawson Bates, arranged with the Attorney General and the Chief Crown Solicitor that the Protestant offenders should be treated leniently. See Paul Bew, Peter Gibbon, Henry Patterson, *The State in Northern Ireland 1921–72*, Manchester 1979, p 91. Bates was always considered to be one of the most partisan of the Unionist ministers, indeed, Sir Henry Wilson, Unionist and former Chief of the imperial general staff, shortly before his assassination by the IRA in London, urged Craig not to appoint him to Home Affairs. Wilson also argued against the establishment of the B-specials (see Bew et al, *op cit*, p 58) yet his spurious reputation for extremism survives even amongst sophisticated commentators; see for example, Vincent Browne's article on Collins, *Sunday Tribune*, 22 August 1992. For the most recent scholarly account, P Hart, 'Michael Collins and the Assassination of Sir Henry Wilson', *Irish Historical Studies*, vol XXXVIII, no 110, November 1992.

[9] Charlemont is referring to the major shift in British policy towards Ireland which begins with the 1881 Land Act.

Increasingly, Britain attempted to deal with Irish grievances by a policy of reform; these were particularly dramatic in the area of land law but also affected large areas of life, in particular Irish education. The London Government was also increasingly unwilling to sponsor in any way sectarian division in Irish life. As late as 20 October 1881, a very senior Liberal, Lord Spencer, felt able to write to Lord Cowper: 'The active support of Orangemen and Protestants is the ultimate resource of English rule in Ireland but ought to be kept until every other card has been played.' In Countess Cowper, *Earl Cowper KC: A Memoir by his Wife*, privately printed, (London) 1913, pp 533–5.

Twenty-two years later a Conservative and Unionist Chief Secretary would claim: 'I had convinced my colleagues, a majority of our supporters in the House . . . that it was right to foster union among Irishmen and to obliterate the vestiges of ancient feuds without troubling ourselves about the ultimate effect of social regeneration on Ireland's attitude towards the 'Home Rule versus Union controversy'. Printed in J W Mackay and Guy Wyndham, *Life and letters of George Wyndham*, London 1925, vol ii, pp 472–3. The divide and rule policy, such as it was, had clearly been abandoned.

[10] The best recent account is undoubtedly A C Hepburn, 'The Belfast Riots of 1935', *Social History*, vol 15, 1990, pp 75–96. Hepburn writes, p 80: 'Whatever the balance of blame for events of the Twelfth, it is clear that the Catholics were more on the receiving end in the days that followed.' See also Bardon, *A History of Ulster*, pp 539–542.

The Belfast riots even made news abroad. On 5 August the *Northern Whig* reported: 'The Frankfurt correspondent of the *Times* states that Dr Goebbels in his speech at Essen, referring to recent events at Belfast, reminded English globetrotters that they need not fly over to Berlin by air to see some smashed Jewish shop windows. As for the alleged unsafe conditions in Germany all sorts of things had happened, but the flag of a foreign country had never been torn from its mast.'

[11] Reverend John Frederick MacNeice. Died 1942. Graduated Trinity College Dublin. Deacon 1895, Priest 1897, Bishop of Cashel and Waterford 1931–1934, Bishop of Down and Connor and Dromore 1935–1942. Father of the poet Louis MacNeice.

[12] Bardon, p 541.

[13] John William Nixon. 1880–1949. Born County Cavan. Alderman for Court Ward Belfast from 1924. Defeated when he stood for North Belfast in 1925. Independent Unionist MP for Woodvale at Stormont from 1929 until his death. Former D I Nixon had been dismissed from the RUC in 1924 after making a very strong speech at an Orange meeting, a figure of some notoriety in Belfast folklore.

[14] Thomas Gibson Henderson. 1887–1970. City Councillor for Shankill from 1918. One of the instigators of the Juvenile Orange Institution of Northern Ireland. Elected to Stormont as an Independent Unionist in North Belfast in 1925. Won the Shankill seat in 1929 which he held until 1953 when he was defeated by an (official) Unionist candidate. Twice defeated when he stood in United Kingdom General Elections.

[15] Possibly Joseph Redmond, fruit grower, Grange House, Annaghmore, Portadown or S A Redmond, JP, farmer and grocer, Kilkinamurray, Dromara, Co Down.

[16] Edward Sullivan Murphy KC. 1880–1945. Unionist MP for City of Londonderry at Stormont 1929–1939. Educated Charterhouse and Trinity College Dublin. Called to the Irish Bar 1903, Inner Temple 1921. Lord Justice of Appeal, Supreme Court of Northern Ireland 1934. Attorney-General for Northern Ireland 1937–1939.

[17] Rev Richard George Salmon King. Died 1958. Dean of Derry from 1921 to 1946. Served as Senior Chaplain to the Forces 36th Division 1914–1916. Late Hon Secretary General Synod of the Church of Ireland.

[18] For a judicious discussion of Brooke's controversial speeches in this epoch, see Brian Barton *Brookeborough: the Making of a Prime Minister*, Belfast 1989, pp 84–89. Interestingly and happily, Brooke himself did not keep his famous advice to employ only 'Protestant lads and lasses' – a Catholic cook was employed at Colebrooke, *The Guardian*, 24 August 1992.

The *Belfast Telegraph*, 20 March 1934 reported: 'A packed gathering of Loyalists listened to stirring speeches by Sir Basil Brooke, Minister of Agriculture, and Mr E S Murphy. This was the Minister's first appearance on a Derry platform and as he rose to speak he was given a real Derry welcome being greeted with loud and prolonged applause.

In his speech, which was punctured with outbursts of cheering, he gave a lucid explanation of the Representation of the People Bill and reiterated his statements regarding the employment by Loyalists of Roman Catholics.'. . .

'The amount of talk and print produced by my statement on the question of disloyal Roman Catholics is phenomenal. I would assure you, however, I have not lost one night's sleep over it. I want to make it perfectly clear that the man I am attacking is the disloyalist (applause). At the last Twelfth of July I said what I did after thinking out the whole question carefully. What I said was justified. I recommend those people who are Loyalists not to employ Roman Catholics, 99% of whom are disloyal. It is not as though I raked this out of the back of my mind without giving full consideration to it. Their own newspaper, in discussing the census themselves, admit that 100% of the Roman Catholics are Nationalists, and, therefore, they are people out for the destruction of the Ulster Constitution.

The Orange Institution is there to defend the Protestant faith and nobody is going to interfere with their faith or their religion. It does not concern us how a man worship[s] his God, but it does concern us when that religion is so politically minded that it is out to destroy us as a body.

What astonishes me is that these people are rather hurt because of my utterances. Study the remarks of the Nationalists! Mr Healy says he is going to do his best to bring the whole of Ulster into the United Ireland by the power of the vote. He means 'peaceful penetration'. Your Nationalist member says the same probably. In the South what can tempt us? O'Duffy thinks we are mugs. In 1922 he said if Ulster would not come in with the South he would use the lead. Well, we can tell him he can try using the lead, but he won't get us in (applause). Mr DeValera says he won't rest content until the foreigners and invaders are driven out of Ireland. That means us. We are not going out of Ireland. Sean O'Kelly says he will set up a Social Catholic State. I don't know what that means, but it sounds very unpleasant. All they have to offer us is the most awful state of chaos that anybody ever produced in this country.

Is it not time they set their own house in order and leave us alone? They are wasting their breath. We are quite content and happy where we are. We are not going to walk into any 'gold brick trap'.

Sir Basil declared: 'Theirs is a mentality we cannot understand. They are foreign to everything we hold to. We are entirely different in sentiments and ideals and pray God we may remain so.'

[19] Captain (later Major) Sir Robert Henry Seymour Dashwood. 1876–1947. Son of 6th Baronet Dashwood. Educated at Wellington, served with 1st Battalion Royal Irish Rifles. Served in First World War 1915–1916, wounded. Twice mentioned in dispatches.

[20] In October 1936 Montgomery received a circular letter from Lady (Cecil) Craigavon appealing for funds to enlarge the Apprentice Boys of Derry Memorial Hall in that city. Montgomery used the opportunity to bring his views home to Lady Craigavon who replied:

'My dear General

I appreciate so much the trouble you took in answering my appeal in such a frank manner. May I be equally frank and say that being an Englishwoman when I first came over here, now 30 years ago, I felt very much as you do. I had many Roman Catholic friends on the other side and in the South of Ireland, and I was quite at a loss to understand the religious feud that existed over here.

I now, however, completely comprehend it, and I am surprised that you, an Ulsterman born and bred, do not also; because, it is not really on religious grounds at all that our people object to their opponents, but because of their insensate disloyalty to the British Throne and Constitution and their constant work and endeavours to get Northern Ireland into what is virtually a Republic in the South. The religious side of it is mere coincidence, the Loyalists happen to be Protestants, and the Disloyalists, Catholics.

Although not an Orangewoman myself I know that the Order, for which I have the most profound respect and admiration, stands for *Civil and religious liberty for all*. I think this is practised by them to a far greater extent than you think. Some of the disturbances that occur occasionally in Belfast are caused by 'riff raff' that neither side would wish to own, and which unfortunately exist in every community. At the same time the Protestants or Loyalists, whichever we like to call them, have in my opinion *every right* to stand up for their principles and the great heritage that has been handed down to them over here; and to oppose the Disloyalists or Roman Catholics, whichever one likes to call them, so long as they continue to work for the disintegration of the United Kingdom. We should not today be enjoying the freedom that we have, if the Apprentice Boys, for whom I am appealing, had not at the time of the Siege taken the stand they did; and it is that same spirit that characterises our people today and has enabled them to successfully overcome the machinations of the disloyal population of Ulster – more power to them!

[21] Professor Robert Mitchell Henry. 1873–1950. Educated Methodist College and Queen's College (later University) Belfast and London University. Professor of Latin 1907–1938. Secretary to the Academic Council QUB. Pro-Vice-Chancellor 1938–1939. Member of the Royal Irish Academy. Professor of Humanity St Andrews University 1939–1947. Author of *The Evolution of Sinn Fein*.

[22] John Miller Andrews. 1871–1956. Company Director. Chairman of Ulster Unionist Labour Association. Stormont MP for Down 1921-1929 and mid-Down 1929–1953. Minister of Labour 1921–1937, Minister of Finance 1937–1940. Prime Minister 1940–1943. High Sheriff of Co Down 1929. Grand Master of Co Down Orange Order from 1941, of Ireland 1948–1954 and Imperial Grand Council of the World 1949–1954.

[23] Sir Joseph Davison. 1868–1948. Alderman in Belfast, retired 1924. A pawnbroker. Knighted 1921. Orange Grand Master of Belfast. NI Senator 1935 until his death in 1948.

[24] William Grant. 1877–1949. Unionist MP at Stormont for North Belfast 1921–1929 and Duncairn 1929–1949. A shipwright by trade. Involved in the founding and training of the UVF. Minister of Public Security in NI 1941–1943, Minister of Labour 1943–1944 and Minister of Health and Local Government from 1944 until his death in 1949.

[25] Brigadier-General Henry George Young. 1870–1956. Educated Harrow and Sandhurst. A professional soldier who served on the North-West Frontier of India (1897–1898), South Africa (1902), and Mesopotamia (1916–1921). Received numerous honours including the DSO (1917) and the Croix de Guerre before retiring from the army in 1921. Serjeant at Arms Northern Ireland Parliament from 1921 to 1951. Older brother of George C G Young MP and Orange County Grand Master for Antrim. In January 1931 the wife of the Rt Hon William Robert Young (eldest of the five Young brothers), herself the daughter of Sir Francis MacNaghten, joined the Irish Association but asked that her name not be published. PRONI D2661/B/7.

[26] Lieutenant-Colonel Alexander Robert Gisborne Gordon DSO DL. 1882–1967. Delamont, Killyleagh. Educated Rugby and Sandhurst. Severely wounded in 1914, subsequently served on staff. Numerous military honours, mentioned in dispatches five times, Croix de Guerre. Retired 1923. Recommissioned served 1940–1942. Unionist MP for East Down at Stormont from 1929 until 1949 when he was succeeded by Brian Faulkner. Minister in Northern Ireland Senate 1951–1961. Speaker 1961–1964. Knighted 1965. President of the Royal Ulster Agricultural Society 1952–1964. In June 1940 resigned his post as a junior minister in the Stormont Government in protest at the general Government inertia and in particular the neglect of civil defence.

[27] Bangor, 6th Viscount. Maxwell Richard Crosbie Ward OBE. 1868–1950. Educated Harrow and Royal Military Academy Woolwich. Retired from army as Major in 1912. Served again 1914–1919, retired as Lieutenant-Colonel. Speaker of the Northern Ireland Senate 1930 until his death in 1950.

[28] Dunleath, 3rd Baron. Charles Henry George Mulholland CBE. 1886–1956. Educated Eton and Sandhurst. Captain in the army, served 1914–1918, awarded DSO 1915. Military Secretary to Lord-Lieutenant of Ireland, Viscount French, 1919–1921. Retired 1921. First wife (Sylvia Henrietta) was Basil Brooke's sister (died 1921). Military Secretary to Governor-General of Australia 1923–1925.

[29] Kilmorey, 4th Earl. Francis Charles Adalbert Henry Needham. 1883–1961. Also Viscount Newry and Mourne. Educated Eton. High Sheriff of Co Down 1913. Served in First World War 1914–1915. Captain RNVR and Commanding Officer of Ulster Division RNVR from 1930 to 1940. HM Lieutenant for Co Down 1949–1959. Great-uncle of Richard Needham, longest serving NIO Minister (6th Earl Kilmorey).

[30] *Northern Whig*, 18 Oct. 1935.

[31] Captain Henry K Dobbs. Monavert, Cushendall, Co Antrim.

[32] Cardinal Joseph Macrory. Archbishop of Armagh. 1861–1945. Born Ballygawley, Co Tyrone. Educated Armagh and Maynooth. Professor Olton College Birmingham 1887–1889, Maynooth 1889–1915. Bishop of Down and Connor 1915–1928. Supporter of Michael Collins but opposed Collins' decision to call off Republican boycott of Belfast goods in January 1922. Represented Northern nationalists at a meeting of the Provisional Government in Dublin later the same month. Strongly opposed Southern recognition of Northern Ireland. Cardinal 1929. Cardinal Macrory refused to take in person an honorary degree offered by Queen's University, Belfast in 1929. In 1931 declared that the Protestant Church in Ireland was 'not even a part of the Church of Christ'. Professor J J Lee, *Government and Politics of Ireland*, Cambridge 1989, p 267, basing himself on the German archives, shows that the Germans believed in 1940 that Macrory was in favour of 'possible German action' to end partition. In a letter dated 12 August 1938 Montgomery wrote to Mary McNeill: 'If you and I had been born of papish parents, I feel sure we should be ardent Catholics; and if Cardinal Macrory had been born a Protestant, he would probably have been a 'County Grandmaster' by now!'. PRONI D2661/B/2

[33] Rev Professor Robert Corkey. 1881–1966. Educated Magee College Londonderry, Queen's College Belfast and Edinburgh University. Minister at Ballygawley 1906–1910. Monaghan 1910–1917. Professor of Ethics in Presbyterian College, Belfast from 1917. Unionist MP for Queen's University at Stormont from 1929 until 1943. Member of Northern Ireland Senate from 1943. Northern Ireland Minister of Education and leader of the Senate 1943–1944.

[34] Colonel John Knox McClintock. 1864–1936. Educated Cheltenham College and Oxford Military College. High Sheriff Co Tyrone 1891. Professional soldier, commanded 3rd Inniskilling Fusiliers 1909–1919. Baronet 1917. County Commandant Co Tyrone Special Constabulary from 1920. CBE 1921. Deputy Lieutenant of Co Tyrone. ADC to the Governor of Northern Ireland.

[35] Sir Herbert Charles Arthur Langham, 13th Bart. 1870–1951. Tempo Manor, Co Fermanagh. Educated Eton. Lieutenant in the army.

[36] John C Crossle. Ballygawley, Co Tyrone. Solicitor and County Grand Master of the Orange Order in Tyrone. A Unionist member of Clogher District Council.

[37] Hugh MacManaway. The Deanery, Enniskillen.

[38] Canon Charles Cullimore. The Rectory, Omagh.

[39] Sir Robert John Lynn. 1873–1945. Editor of the *Northern Whig* 1913–1928. Unionist MP at Stormont. Represented West Belfast from 1921 to 1929 when multi-member seats were abolished (with the exception of Queen's University). Subsequently represented North Antrim from 1929 until his death in 1945. Represented Woodvale (Belfast) at Westminster 1918–1922 and West Belfast from 1922 to 1929.

[40] Hugh Montgomery Irwin. Derrygore, Enniskillen. A Unionist candidate for Fermanagh and Tyrone (Westminster) 1931. Defeated by Joe Devlin and Cahir Healy.

[41] Captain T T H Verschoyle 1894–1993. Large Protestant land owner from Co Fermanagh. cf. B Barton, *Brookeborough*, pp 79–81. When Verschoyle died early in 1993 the *Belfast Telegraph* printed the following obituary:
'World war veteran Major Terence Verschoyle – a former High Sheriff of Co Fermanagh, has died. He was 98 years old. Descending from a family who left the Netherlands as the result of religious persecution in 1568, Major Verschoyle's grandfather was rector of Derryvullan North (Irvinestown) from 1865–1891. A son of Mr Stuart Joseph Verschoyle, Tullycleagh House, Ballinamallard, he was educated at Rugby, then the Imperial College of Science and Technology, and London University where he graduated in the degree of Doctor of Philosophy in 1926. He worked for some time as a research chemist with ICI.
  Following command of the Ulster Volunteer Force in the Ballinamallard area in 1912 he enlisted in the Royal Inniskilling Fusiliers, serving throughout the First World War. He was twice mentioned in dispatches, was awarded the Military Cross in 1918 and in that year received the Knight of the Order of the Crown of Italy decoration.
  On returning home he farmed in Tullycleagh – and was appointed a deputy Lieutenant for Co Fermanagh in 1920. He officiated as a Justice of the Peace in the inter-war years. He was High Sheriff of Co Fermanagh in 1929, served on the Fermanagh County Council as an Ulster Unionist, and was involved in Church of Ireland work. A keen huntsman, he was actively associated with the Fermanagh Harriers Hunt Club. Having joined the Reserve of Officers he rejoined the Army following the outbreak of war in 1939 and after the war settled in England.' (*Belfast Telegraph*, 7 January 1993)
  Verschoyle responded to Basil Brooke's Newtownbutler speech appealing to loyalists 'wherever possible, to employ Protestant lads and lassies' by saying: 'He who sows the wind shall reap the whirlwind . . . it remains to be seen whether the Colebrooke Hitler will receive a well-merited rebuke from a responsible member of the government.' (Quoted in Barton, p 538)

[42] James P Burkitt. Laragh, Ballinamallard, Co Fermanagh. County Surveyor. and distinguished naturalist – father of the celebrated medic Burkitt later became a member of the Irish Association.

[43] For Protestant Home Rulers, see James Loughlin, 'The Irish Protestant Home Rule Association and Nationalist Politics 1886–1893', in *Irish Political Studies*, vol 24, 1984–1985, pp 341–360, J R B McMinn *Against the Tide: J. B. Armour, Irish Presbyterian Minister and Home Ruler*, Belfast 1985.

[44] On this difficult period and time see 'Tales of the RIC', *Blackwood's Magazine*, October–December 1921, pp 610–638. For a more academic view, see Paul Bew, 'Sinn Fein, Agrarian Radicals and the War of Independence 1919–1921', in D G Boyce (ed), *Revolution in Ireland*, London 1989.

[45] Cahir Healy. Nationalist MP for Fermanagh and Tyrone in 1925 and for South Fermanagh at Stormont from 1929 to 1965. Elected to represent Fermanagh and Tyrone at Westminster in 1922 and 1923 Healy was interned by the Unionist Government from May 1922 until February 1924. Healy stood for a Westminster seat for the same area in a by-election in 1931 and retained it in the General Election of the same year and won Fermanagh/South Tyrone again in 1950 and 1951. See the excellent treatment in Eamon Phoenix's forthcoming book on Northern nationalism, Belfast 1993, Ulster Historical Foundation.

[46] Rev William Shaw Kerr. 1873–1960. Educated Dublin University. Rector of Banbridge 1916–1932. Archdeacon of Dromore 1929–1932. Dean of St Anne's Cathedral, Belfast 1932–1945. Bishop of Down and Dromore 1944–1955.

[47] Sir Dudley Evelyn Bruce McCorkell. 1883–1960. Educated Shrewsbury and Pembroke College Cambridge. High Sheriff of Londonderry 1925. Mayor of Londonderry 1929–1934. Knighted 1933. Chairman of Wm McCorkell & Co Ltd, Londonderry Port and Harbour Commissioner. Director of Bank of Ireland, Co Donegal Railways and Londonderry Gaslight Company. HM Lieutenant for Londonderry 1957.

[48] Sir Basil Alexander Talbot McFarland, 2nd Baronet. 1898–1986. High Sheriff of Londonderry 1930–1938 and 1952. Mayor of Londonderry 1939 and 1945–1950. Lieutenant for the City of Londonderry 1939–1975. Partner in Henry Lane and Co. Director of several companies including Londonderry Gaslight Co and Londonderry and Lough Swilly Railway Co 1946–1981. Member of Unemployment Assistance Board Northern Ireland to 1939. Served in both World Wars. ADC (Additional) to The King 1950–1952, to The Queen 1952–1960. Irish Rugby International 1920–1922. On 3 December 1971 terrorists broke into the home of Sir Basil McFarland and planted a gelignite bomb which caused extensive damage. The Official IRA later issued a statement claiming responsibility and saying that Sir Basil's home had been bombed and burned, 'as a retaliatory action for the wrecking of republican and civilian homes by the British army.' Sir Basil (then aged 73) could be considered lucky to have been away at the time of the attack, nine days later Unionist Senator Jack Barnhill was murdered by the Official IRA when he tried to prevent them burning his home.

[49] At the 1935 UK General Election (14 November) Fermanagh and Tyrone returned two Nationalists who refused to take their Westminster seats.

P Cunningham	N	50,891	26.2%
A Mulvey	N	50,603	26.1%
R E Dean	U	46,625	24.0%
J M Blakiston-Houston	U	46,000	23.7%
Turnout 82.4%			

According to the recent research of Mr Enda Staunton, graduate student in the Department of Politics, Queen's University Belfast, Blakiston-Houston complained to Sir Basil Brooke about the failure of local Unionists to seek Catholic support. Blakiston-Houston had been pursuing a military career outside Ireland and Brooke felt that he was simply out of touch with local realities.

50 Sir Alexander Wilson Hungerford. 1884–1969. Secretary of the Ulster Unionist Council 1921–1941. Stormont MP for Oldpark 1929–1945. Parliamentary Secretary to Ministries of Commerce, Home Affairs and Health and Local Government 1941–1944. Chief Whip 1944–1945. Member of Senate 1948–1957.

51 Sir Robert John Kennedy. 1851–1936. Educated Harrow and University College Oxford. Married a daughter of 5th Viscount Bangor (Bertha Ward). Entered Diplomatic Service 1874. Secretary of embassy in Spain, Turkey and Russia. Charge d'affaires in Bulgaria, Romania and Persia. HM Minister in Montenegro 1893, Envoy to Uruguay 1906. Retired 1912. High Sheriff of Co Down 1915. A Governor of Campbell College, Belfast. Director in Chief Ulster British Red Cross and Order of St John from 1915.

52 Sir Richard Dawson Bates. 1876–1949. A Belfast solicitor. Secretary of the Ulster Unionist Council 1906–1921. Responsible for the organisation of the Ulster Covenant in 1912. Knighted 1921. Baronetcy 1937. Stormont MP for East Belfast 1921–1929 and Victoria 1929–1943. First Minister of Home Affairs at Stormont 1921–1943. A hard line Unionist described by a critic of the Unionist Party as: 'A small man, physically and intellectually . . . . His great strength was his meticulous attention to detail. . . . he was the grey eminence of Ulster Unionism who remained in the shadow of Carson and Craig.' J F Harbinson, *The Ulster Unionist Party 1882–1973*, pp 50–51, Blackstaff, Belfast 1973.

53 Lt Col Sir Charles George Wickham. 1879–1971. Educated Harrow and the Royal Military College, Sandhurst. Entered the army 1899, Captain 1906, Major 1915. Served in South Africa 1900–1902, Europe 1914–1916 and as part of the British military expedition in Siberia after the Russian revolution. Numerous military distinctions including French Legion of Honour, Order of the Crown of Italy and Czechoslovak War Cross. Divisional Commissioner of Royal Irish Constabulary 1920. Knighted 1922. Inspector-General of the RUC 1922–1945. Major General in the Home Guard during World War II. Head of British Police-Prison mission to Greece 1945–1952. Formed Ulster Special Constabulary in 1920 and the RUC in 1922, also Ulster Home Guard in 1940. High Sheriff of Co Down 1960 and Deputy Lieutenant for Co Down 1962.

54 Sir John Milne Barbour. 1868–1951. Educated at Harrow and Brasenose College, Oxford. Managing Director of several textile companies. High Sheriff of Co Antrim 1905, Co Down 1907. Stormont MP for Antrim 1921–1929, South Antrim 1929–1951. Minister of Commerce 1925–1941. Minister of Finance 1941–1943. Baronetcy 1943.

55 Hugh MacDowell Pollock. 1852–1937. Stormont MP for South Belfast 1921–1929 and Windsor, Belfast 1929–1937. Minister of Finance in the

Northern Ireland Government 1921–1937. Pollock's views, which were closer to Charlemont's than to those of Dawson Bates, are discussed at length in Paul Bew, Peter Gibbon, Henry Patterson, *The State in Northern Ireland 1921–1972*, Manchester 1979, chapter 3.

56 Rt Hon Sir Robert William Hugh O'Neill. 1883–1982. 1st Baron Rathcavan (1953). Educated Eton and New College Oxford. Bar, Inner Temple 1909. Contested Stockport 1906. Served France and Palestine 1915–1918. Major in army. Unionist MP at Westminster for Mid-Ulster 1915–1922, for Co Antrim 1922–1950 and North Antrim 1950–1952. MP for Co Antrim at Stormont 1921–1929. First Speaker of Northern Ireland House of Commons 1921–1929. Chairman of Conservative Private Members (1922) Committee 1935–1939. Parliamentary Under-Secretary of State for India and for Burma 1939–1940. HM Lieutenant for Co Antrim 1949–1959. Father of Phelim O'Neill later Minister of Education and Minister of Agriculture at Stormont.

57 This is a reference to the school of Fivemiletown, established and supported as an 'integrated' school by the Montgomery family.

58 Rev James Godfrey MacManaway. 1898–1951. Educated Campbell College Belfast and Trinity College Dublin. Served in the Cavalry and RAF 1914–1918. Ordained 1923. Served in WWII becoming Chaplain of 10 Corps. Unionist MP for the City of Londonderry from 1947 (by-election) until 1951 when he resigned. At the centre of a political storm when he was elected to represent West Belfast at Westminster in 1950 but was subsequently disqualified because he was a Church of Ireland minister.

59 On this topic see, for background, Denis Kennedy, *The Widening Gulf: Northern Attitudes to the Independent Irish State 1919–1949*, Belfast 1988.

60 The reference here is to *Round Table*, vol 26, 1936/37, p 802. 'The manner in which the revision of the constituencies helped the Fianna Fail Party is proved by the fact that while they secured a seat for every 8,816 valid votes the other parties taken together required 12,083 votes for each seat won. The Independent candidates, who should have secured 13 seats in proportion to the number of votes they obtained, suffered most from this gerrymandering.'

61 The Northern Ireland government's approach was demonstrated by its continuation of such relief schemes after they had been forbidden by the London Treasury: it seems that both communities benefited. See Paul Bew 'A Protestant Parliament and a Protestant State. Some reflections on Government and Minority in Ulster 1921–1943', in Art Cosgrave and J McGuire, *Parliament and Community*, Historical Studies, XIV, Belfast 1983, pp 237–248.

62 Letters from General Hugh Montgomery to Miss Mary McNeill. PRONI D2661/B/2.

63 Correspondence between General Hugh Montgomery and Father John McShane of Omagh PRONI D3480/51. It has been pointed out to us by Mr Patrick Maume that Michael O Cuinneagain (son of Patrick Cunningham, Nationalist MP at Westminster for Fermanagh and Tyrone

between 1935 and 1950) recalls Fr McShane as a strong Republican and opponent of anti-Catholic discrimination by the local council, with a fervent devotion to Blessed Oliver Plunkett both as religious and political martyr. McShane was said to have been passed over for the Bishopric of Derry in 1939 because of his outspoken political views, and the newly appointed Bishop Farren transferred him to Buncrana in the Donegal section of the diocese to get him out of the way. Michael O Cuinneagain, *Partition from Michael Collins to Bobby Sands* (Tantallon, Donegal Town, 1986) pp 98–100. Benedict Kiely (*Drink to the Bird*), London 1991, remembers MacShane as an intellectural and antiquarian, with an interest in local memorials of Penal days.

[64] McShane here fails to mention that Redmond was offered a Cabinet post at the same time but felt he had to turn it down.

[65] PRONI D627/A/2/130–140.